TEACHING KIDS
THE BASICS
OF LITURGY

making the rituals
more meaningful

TEACHING KIDS
THE BASICS
OF LITURGY

making the rituals
more meaningful

Robert D. Duggan

ThomasMore®
– An RCL Company –
Allen, Texas

Send all inquiries to:
THOMAS MORE PUBLISHING
An RCL Company
200 East Bethany Drive
Allen, Texas 75002-3804

E-mail: **www.RCLweb.com**

Bookstores:
> Call Christian Distribution Services 888-444-2524
> Fax 615-793-5973

Individuals, parishes, and schools:
> Call Thomas More Publishing 800-822-6701
> Fax 800-688-8356

International:
> Fax Thomas More Publishing 972-264-3719

Printed in the United States of America

Library of Congress Catalog Number 00132875

ISBN 0-88347-409-3

1 2 3 4 5   04 03 02 01 00

TABLE OF CONTENTS

Introduction

A mong my earliest childhood memories, and those I cherish most, are several recollections of being in church with my mother: making a visit to the blessed Sacrament for a few minutes on an afternoon shopping trip, and her carefully explaining what the flickering red light beside the tabernacle was all about; my fidgeting with impatience while she fingered her beads, until she let me explore her fat prayer book, stuffed with holy cards and other fascinating memorabilia that held me spellbound; her showing me how to genuflect properly, proving that I could do it just as well as the big kids.

I remember slipping into a back pew of our parish church with her on a wintry afternoon, while the parochial school kids were engaged in some sort of ceremony that I had never before seen (I was not yet of school age), and being absolutely thunderstruck with feelings of awe and wonder, as incense clouds filled the air, and a swelling chorus of *Tantum ergo* echoed in the cavernous, vaulted, ceiling overhead. Years later, my scholarly reading led me to Rudolf Otto's phrase *mysterium fascinans et tremendum* to describe our encounter with the transcendent. I knew what he was referring to, because I could remember the feelings stirred in my very body in that dark church, as I watched a mysterious ritual whose meaning I surely could not comprehend, but whose depth and seriousness I intuited, and whose allure was as powerful as anything I had ever encountered.

Not all of my "religious experiences" were equally uplifting, of course. I recall also my first "crisis of faith" shortly before making my First Holy Communion. Somehow or other, I had gotten the idea that one of the "proofs" that the bread and wine truly becomes the body and blood of Jesus was the predictable "miracle of the bells." It was the angels, I was convinced, who were responsible for the pealing of bells at the words of consecration. I used to anticipate the miracle and tremble in awe at the regularity of this heavenly intervention, this incredible sign of divinity present in our midst Sunday after Sunday. When the family sat up front one Sunday, and I had a line of sight that allowed me to see the altar boy reach down and pick up the handbells at the Consecration, it was as if Toto had suddenly pulled aside the curtain in the Emerald Palace, revealing the Wizard in all of his humanity. If not the angels, then is it *all* a sham? I forget whether I had the courage to ask any adult about this shattering revelation. What I do remember is the confusion and shame I felt at having been so foolish a believer, so naive as to think that angels were doing a task that altar boys, in fact, performed. Somehow or other— perhaps by another miracle of divine grace—my faith in the real presence was sufficiently restored for me to make that First Holy Communion some weeks later, with nary a doubt about the veracity of transubstantiation.

I grew up in the 1940s and 1950s, the child of practicing Catholic parents, who when shopped for a new house, first had to determine that there was room in the neighborhood parochial school for all of the kids in the family. And they told the realtor showing them around that the house should preferably be within walking distance of the church and school. I grew up in a world of stable religious symbols, part of a worshipping community that boasted of the unchanging nature of its liturgical tradition, in a ghetto Catholicism for whom Latin was the language of the divine, and in which rubrical exactitude and precision were sure signs of holiness.

Thousands of dedicated nuns carefully schooled the likes of me in arcane religious information, such as the complexities of fasting regulations during Lent and the significance of rose-colored vestments on Gaudete and Laetare Sundays. The culture around me reinforced at every point the traditional pieties of our Catholic way of prayer and worship, from the family rosary for the conversion of Russia, to the wearing of scapulars that guaranteed a happy death, to the correct response and posture for virtually every moment of the Sunday Mass. We were initiated into a ritual code of conduct and a specialized language of prayer that was extremely sophisticated and nuanced, even in the "watered down" version that was given to the very young. Religious literacy, in the sense of familiarity with the theological jargon in which the basic tenets of the faith were expressed, was widespread and remarkably high. So, too, was knowledge of the religious "code language" that our symbol system represented. Catholics *knew* how to genuflect and what the mysteries of the Rosary were; they *knew* the matter and form of each of the seven sacraments, and they could tell you whether Septuagesima came before or after Sexuagesima.

In the cultural upheavals of the 1960s and 1970s, all of this changed. It is easy to romanticize the past, to create nostalgia for an idealized recollection that forgets the flaws and shortcomings and imagines all was rosy in the good old days. But my portrayal of so much that was wonderful about my own childhood formation in faith is in no way intended to lament the fact that things are different now. Rather, it is simply to remind us how different the world of children today really is from that of a previous generation. Those who blame the Second Vatican Council for the loss of so much that they cherished in the Church have, I believe, too narrow an understanding of the relationship between cultural and religious change. The fact is, in the last half of the twentieth century, virtually every major social institution (the Church included) underwent profound changes in response to political, economic, cultural, and technological transformations that were unprecedented both in their scale and in their rapidity.

The Second Vatican Council, I firmly believe, was providentially guided by the Holy Spirit so that the Church could be part of that era of transformation, not as its victim, but in a proactive way that would make of it a credible voice, capable of proclaiming the Gospel to the twenty-first century with all of the vigor and relevance of the "new Pentecost" for which Pope John XXIII had us pray. With stunning rapidity, a religious organization with two thousand years of history renewed virtually its entire system of prayer and worship. The wonder is not that a tiny fraction of disgruntled followers of Archbishop Lefebvre should have broken away, nor that among older Catholics there is some nostalgia for "how it used to be," nor even that there are younger Catholics who never knew the Tridentine Church but nonetheless long to return to it. Rather, I judge the miracle of our times to be the fact that, in massive numbers, Catholics have embraced the liturgical changes of Vatican II, and have begun with enthusiasm the deeper work of renewal for which those revised rites call. Throughout our country and around the world, faithful Catholics are learning a new vocabulary of worship and beginning to internalize the spirit beneath the new forms of prayer mandated by Vatican II. Despite the "bumps" along the way, liturgical reform and renewal is an irreversible fact of life. The regressive and reactionary forces in our Church that sometimes get disproportionate notice in the media can in no way compare to the providential springtime of liturgical renewal that appears in the vast majority of communities and households everywhere.

This little book is meant to help those who have the sacred task of helping the young to be part of the providential awakening of the Church that the Second Vatican Council set in motion. If you are a teacher of religion, whether in the classroom of a Catholic school, in a parish religious education program, in a children's catechumenal process, or within the "domestic church" of your own family, this resource is meant to help and guide you in the exercise of your responsibility to the next generation.

I do not wish to minimize the scope of the challenge you face.

The coherent Catholic culture that I knew in my childhood has gone, certainly not to be restored in the foreseeable future, and perhaps never to return. Ours is a world of diversity, and our Catholic Church reflects that pluralism in every respect. To make matters even more difficult, today's parents and teachers who grew up immediately after the Council were often deprived of so much of our rich tradition of prayer and worship, as their elders threw out the baby with the bath water, neglecting to pass on much of the value from the past, in favor of the latest fad or whatever was "new." Those elders are the grandparents of today; and even as many of them lament and attempt to retrieve some of what they have too long neglected, they find themselves confused over what they lost that was valuable and worth restoring, and what elements of the renewal really were important and must be passed on to their grandchildren. Thus, the two generations that by right should be poised confidently to pass on to the young a living tradition of Catholic prayer and worship, often find themselves at a loss.

This book is meant to offer a solid framework, a truly renewed liturgical vision in the spirit of Vatican II, that will indicate just what is most important to teach today's children about our liturgical tradition. The contents thoroughly reflect the spirit of the liturgical renewal that has unfolded since the close of the Council. Busy working mothers may no longer be able to slip into the last pew on a winter afternoon with their young child to explain the flickering red candle beside the tabernacle. But for concerned Catholic parents and teachers whose children still question "What's that?" or "Why do we . . .?" the present volume contains a wealth of information that is an accurate and reliable guide to the basics about Catholic prayer and worship.

As pastor of a busy suburban parish, I often have occasion to interact with young children around issues touching on our liturgical life. Whether during interviews prior to First Communion or Confirmation, while visiting classes in the parish religious education program or in the local Catholic school, or in the many other contexts in which I observe and interact with the young,

Robert D. Duggan

I am constantly struck by the critical need for them to have a mastery of the basics about our tradition of prayer and worship. When I see a ten-year-old who does not know how to genuflect, or a seventh grader who does not know how to bless himself or herself; when I ask about the tabernacle and its contents and the fourth graders aren't sure just what it's about, then I am reminded of the urgency of our task. Together, we need to work hard to see to it that our children enjoy a basic literacy about our Catholic way of prayer and worship. Pastors, catechists, school teachers and parents need to share a consensus as to what those basics are and how they are to be explained as part of a "renewed" liturgical vision. The Second Vatican Council certainly *did not* change the core truths of our faith. But it certainly *did* change the way we worship, and the bishops at the Council were clear and insistent on the pedagogical task that must accompany our renewed liturgical experience over the long haul.

This book represents a summary of those basics with which I would want every child in my parish to be familiar by the time she or he is ready for high school. Not all of it is important for a first grader to know; a child will not be ready for some of the information until third grade, some in sixth, and so on. I leave it to those who know each child best to determine when or what part of a topic can be covered at each developmental stage. Nor do I attempt here to offer pedagogical techniques or child-appropriate language that fits various stages of growth. My audience is the adult person who is entrusted with the gift of a child of God, a child whose questions are so often profoundly religious and who invariably seeks to know and understand better the world in which she or he is living and growing.

This material is not meant to serve in any way as a curriculum or course of study. It is meant to clarify and remind parents and teachers just what the latest and best thinking in the Church says about our ancient tradition of prayer and worship. Much of it will be familiar, I would hope. Some may be brand new information, while other sections may clarify what was familiar but had become confused or forgotten. In every case, it is my hope that learning about our Catholic way of approaching God in prayer helps to deepen and intensify one's relationship with Jesus Christ, who *is* our "endless liturgy" before God's throne.

At the most profound level, our liturgy is about a mystery of love, love that embraces a God who has become one with our human flesh, an ineffable God who can be approached only haltingly, and whom we see only darkly, as in a mirror. In rituals whose roots were already ancient in the time of Jesus, as well as in liturgical forms as contemporary as our own generation, we Catholics offer praise and thanksgiving to the God of love who has revealed to children what is hidden from the wise and the learned. As we school our children in the ways of prayer and in the wonderful richness of our Catholic way of worship, may they—and we—be led more and more surely into the mystery of that God of infinite love.

1

GOD'S HOUSE IS A HOUSE
FOR THE CHURCH

The Notion of Sacred Space

All of us have had experiences of "sacred space," places that we experience as "holy" because they radiate a particular sense of the divine presence. Sometimes those places are fleeting—a broad meadow glistening with raindrops after a spring shower, with a rainbow dancing overhead. And sometimes those places enjoy a permanency that is tied to the aura of holiness that fills the space—as in a vaulted burial chamber of a Roman catacomb. Religious shrines dot the globe, and virtually every culture has places that are considered sacred. Magnificent temples to the Buddha, St. Peter's Basilica in Rome, the great pyramids of the Aztecs in Mexico, the healing waters of Lourdes, these are the kinds of places where devotees and even casual tourists encounter a sacred presence that is as palpable as it is elusive.

But sacred space is not limited to edifices or vistas that overwhelm with their sheer size or artistic accomplishment. Each of us also knows of ordinary places that have been made holy by what has happened in them. A bed that has been passed down in a family for generations, where both births and deaths have occurred, can often be a sacred space that connects us to a mystery far beyond our ability to put into words. A grotto where we received great consolation in prayer, or the corner of a favorite room where we know we can always retreat into solitude, these are the kinds of ordinary places that can become sacred space by virtue of what transpires there.

Christian tradition has a history of sacred space that is intimately tied to the ways that we have come to know our God in prayer. That history is not a simple one, however. For example, among the writings of the Christian Apologists of the early centuries, there is a surviving text in which the author boasts to his pagan audience that, unlike other religions of the day, Christians have neither altars nor temples. It was a matter of pride, it seems, that the early Christian community did not localize the sacred in the places of worship that their neighbors associated with the divine presence.

In fact, one can even find a kind of bias against liturgical ritual in some of the earliest Christian texts. In reaction to the perceived legalism of Judaism and the indiscriminant polytheism of the Roman Empire, Christians were proud to be unencumbered by ritual trappings that they considered empty display. In the writings of St. Paul, the liturgical language of "offering" and "sacrifice" is no longer used in reference to ceremonies that take place in shrines or temples. Rather, a Christian's whole life is seen as the acceptable sacrifice that is offered to God: "I urge you, therefore, brothers, by the mercies of God, to offer your bodies as a living sacrifice, holy and pleasing to God, your spiritual worship." (Romans 12:1) It is one's everyday life of obedience to God's will, not the offering of ritual sacrifices in some designated "holy place" that constitutes true "worship" for Paul.

We know, of course, that from the very beginning, believers in Jesus gathered on the Lord's Day in commemoration of his resurrection, to share a fellowship meal at which the Scriptures were read and interpreted, and to pray a blessing over bread and wine in memory of him. Those gatherings were held not in temple or synagogues, but in the homes of members of the community. Often out of necessity for fear of persecution, Christians kept secret the places in which they gathered. But we have evidence that even before the era of persecution had ended, certain places began to be set aside for the exclusive use of the Christian community's prayer. Archaeologists have unearthed "house churches" in which bathing pools have clearly been decorated for use as baptisteries, and in which a larger gathering space has been created by removing the wall to an adjoining room so that the community could gather to share Word and meal together.

After Constantine gave his official support to Christianity in the fourth century, a large number of churches were built all over the Empire. It is interesting, however, that the architectural form which was "borrowed" to construct those places for the worship of the Christian community was the *basilica*, a secular meeting-hall, not the familiar temples of the pagan cults, nor the synagogues of the Jews. Nonetheless, before long grandiose embellishment began to characterize those newly constructed places of Christian worship and gave them an aura much more of sacred space than of a secular meeting-hall.

What this brief look at the early history of Christian buildings tells us is that the physical space in which Christians gather for worship has, from the beginning, been characterized by a degree of ambivalence. On the one hand, the earliest strata of Christian experience wished to move away from the notion of a localized place where the deity is worshiped/housed. Instead, their freedom to gather for prayer in homes or even by the bank of a river was a bold action that "de-sacralized" the notion of temple/cultic shrine as the privileged place for contact with God. By his incarnation, Jesus the Son of God made all of creation "holy," and so his followers did not need to go to a "sacred place" to worship. Jesus said it was "neither on this mountain nor in Jerusalem" that his followers would worship God, but "true worshipers will worship the Father in spirit and truth." (John 4:21, 23) But on the other hand, it seems that despite this viewpoint, the early Christians were not exempt from a kind of anthropological "inevitability" in their impulse to identify places considered "holy" because they localized one's encounter with the divine.

These two strands of Christian tradition need not compete with each other. Rather than remain in tension, one can see them as complementary aspects of a richly multi-faceted sense of the sacred. Children need to be exposed to and become comfortable with both ways of encountering sacred space. Another way of expressing this is to say that children should learn that the building we call a church is both God's house and the house of God's people. They can be introduced to this two-fold perspective even as they learn the meaning of the word "church." The root meaning of the term refers, of course, to the community of disciples themselves. Only later in history did the word also come to designate the building in which the community gathered for worship, the building that naturally came to be seen as "God's house."

The tradition that sees the church as a house for God's people places emphasis on the community and its sacred actions (i.e., of worship) as the source for the "holiness" of the place. From this perspective, a church is holy, first and foremost, because of what we do there, not because of what we have there. This is in no way meant to downplay the importance of the reserved Sacrament. It is simply to acknowledge that what we "have" (the blessed

Sacrament) is the result of what we "do" (celebrate the Eucharist). The action of celebration is primary in the sense that it is the source whence comes the gift of the blessed Sacrament.

The tradition that sees the church as a kind of temple/shrine stresses that it is the presence of a sacred object that renders a place sacred. While we are not exempt from that archetypal intuition of the sacred, we also recognize that the "object" of our devotion is the blessed Sacrament, a person whose presence is that of a living "thou," not that of an inanimate cultic object. Children can and should easily grasp that on both accounts—because of the presence of God in the actions of the community that gathers as the body of Christ, and because of the presence of God in the blessed Sacrament reserved there—the building we call "church" is considered sacred space. Presented in this way, the two perspectives are complementary, not in competition. The church is both God's house and the house of God's people.

Helping children to grasp this two-fold, complementary perspective on sacred space is made easier if they have been exposed to a similar dynamic within their own home. Children should be given a sense of the sacredness of everyday family life from a very early age. The regular routine of prayer that punctuates the daily and weekly life of the home should be the normal occasion for instilling in children an awareness of God's presence in all that we do. Prayer in the morning and at bedtime, prayer at meals and on special occasions, prayer that comes effortlessly to one's lips in myriad situations, such prayer that becomes the fabric of one's life is the way that a child knows "from within" that God is part of every part of what we do. That same awareness should be fostered in a school setting, where the teacher constantly invokes God's presence in prayer as a regular dimension of the classroom experience.

In addition, however, children should be exposed to the experience of a "sacred place" by creating their own special places of prayer and worship, both at home and in the classroom. That is the purpose of a holy picture of a guardian angel above one's bed, or a crucifix on the wall, or a statue of Mary in a special place of honor. Children delight in placing flowers at a homemade shrine to Mary during May or October, or drawing a picture of their patron saint on their nameday to be displayed in their very own "prayer corner."

Parents and teachers who give to children a lively sense of the sacred which resides within our everyday activities, as well as in special places set apart, will find it an easy matter to introduce the idea that a church is sacred in the same two ways. Children will have no difficulty understanding that this place is sacred because in it God's holy people gather to read God's Word and celebrate the Eucharist in fulfillment of the command of Jesus. Likewise, they will easily grasp the holiness of a place that is filled with the religious symbols of our faith, above all, the tabernacle as a special place of reservation and prayer.

One's awareness of the nature of any given place dictates what is appropriate behavior in that place. Children quickly learn that one does not shout out in the middle of a concert or restaurant. They know also that we greet people in our homes with warm hospitality and words of welcome. So, too, children need to understand the importance of an atmosphere of hospitality and welcome in a church that wishes to reverence the stranger as one in whom we encounter the Christ. And, in the same way, they need to understand that when the holy people of God are about the task of worship, there are very specific behaviors that are called for and that convey respect for the holiness both of the place and of what is happening within it. Both joyful shouts of "Alleluia" during the celebration of the Eucharist and profound silence before the blessed Sacrament are appropriate. Both conversation and quiet can be legitimate ways that a child learns to reverence the holy presence of a sacred space.

The Church Gives Shape to Our Faith

Imagine a society in which the vast majority of Christians are illiterate, where only a tiny handful of people own bibles, and where there are no catechisms, religion textbooks, or other documents offering an explanation of our Catholic faith. In that society there are no posters or billboards or reproductions of great works of religious art, no electronic media that can summon up visual images on command to enrich the religious imagination. There are no schools or religion classes that instruct children in the truths of religion, no public libraries where the curious can seek answers to their questions or find out about their ancestors in the Faith.

Such a society is not the stuff of a science fiction novel set in a post-nuclear holocaust era. Rather, such a society was the everyday reality of believers during the majority of the Christian centuries prior to our own. How, then, was faith passed on? How were children and adults schooled in the truths of divine revelation, given knowledge of the Gospel and Jesus' promise of salvation? How were the stories of saints and sinners, of grace and redemption passed from generation to generation without the enormous resources that we take for granted today? The answer lies in an ancient adage that "the liturgy is the *school of faith*." By "liturgy" here, of course, we must understand both all of the rituals of prayer and worship and those who participate in them, as well as the very building that houses those sacred actions.

In previous generations before the advent of our modern catechetical enterprise, the traditions of the Church were passed down as part of a living experience of faith, in families and in communities for whom the local church provided meaning and guidance to their lives. In such a society, the "sacred texts" from which they learned about the Christian faith were not bound volumes. Rather, the texts that they read were the buildings (churches) they recognized as sacred space, as well as the sacred actions (the liturgy) that took place in those buildings. People in such societies had a keen ability to read and understand the symbols of faith that surrounded them in church, just as today's young people display a remarkably sophisticated "computer literacy" that often leaves their elders amazed.

Our contemporary biases regarding how children should be taught about their Catholic tradition of faith often result in a failure to show them how they can learn from our most ancient and most basic "school of faith." The remaining pages of this chapter offer a kind of "tour" of the church building, seen as a sourcebook from which the Christian faith can be learned. The sacred space that is our church building, the objects and embellishments that are found there, all speak in symbolic fashion about the deep truths of our Christian belief. Adults must be conversant with this visual language of faith so that they, in turn, can initiate the young into the richness that it contains.

The Arrangement of the Sacred Space

The entire confines of a church should be recognized as "sacred space." The sheer volume of the place where the people of God assemble is a powerful statement about the primacy of the community that gathers there. We need to be careful not to convey to children the idea that the sanctuary area is the "sacred" part of the church (which would, of course, then imply the opposite about the place where the people gather). The separation of the sanctuary space is a reflection of the hierarchical nature of Christian worship, not a suggestion that there are "holy" individuals who occupy that space, while the "unwashed" are kept at a distance. Rather, the sanctuary is a space set aside for those who preside over the sacred action of the assembly and for those who exercise specialized ministries within it (e.g., the proclamation of the Word). But the entire space—the nave in which the community gathers and the sanctuary in which the ministers function—is made holy by the presence of the gathered church, by the body of Christ, and by the holy actions (praise, thanksgiving, petition, intercession, and so forth) that they perform.

Church documents call for a particular arrangement of certain elements of the furnishings within the church. This is done sometimes as a practical matter and sometimes as a theological statement about specific relationships that characterize the participants in the liturgical action. The rituals for each of the sacraments spell out how those spatial arrangements, especially among individuals, embody significant relationships. Our Roman Catholic liturgy gives a great deal of prominence to processions, and so often it is important to observe *who* goes from one place to another and *why* that is done. It is significant, for example, that the gifts for Eucharist are carried forward by members of the assembly and presented to the presider. The bread, wine, and monetary offering could be delivered to where they are needed in other ways, to be sure. But the explicit direction that they be carried in procession *from the assembly* to the presider is a way of saying something important about our whole theology of eucharistic offering. Another obvious example of an important spatial direction is the stipulation that the one who presides at the Eucharist should sit in a chair that expresses his office of directing the assembly's prayer. The rubrics insist that "every appearance of a throne should be avoided," (GIRM, 271) to make it clear that the presider does not "Lord it over them." (Matthew 20:25) Rather, the one who presides functions *in persona Christi,* and thus he acts as a servant of the assembly and its prayer, not as an earthly ruler looking down on his subjects. (Cf. Matthew 20:20-28)

Children, like the rest of the assembly, will unconsciously absorb the message of the way that a church is arranged. But it is important to help them name what is significant about a church and its furnishings, about the arrangement of the objects and of the people who make up our worship. Pointing out to them the subtle cues that are implicit in such arrangements is an important way of heightening their "symbolic literacy" and showing them how to read the language of our sacred spaces.

The Assembly

Liturgical theologians today refer to the assembly itself as the primary symbol of God's holy presence in our midst. This way of speaking is as ancient as the theology of St. Paul's letters, where he teaches, "Do you not know that your body is a temple of the Holy Spirit within you . . . ?" (1 Corinthians 6:19) In chapter 3 of the same letter, where the context is the church that he founded at Corinth, he uses the identical image in reference to the entire community of believers: "Do you not know that you are the temple of God, and that the Spirit of God dwells in you?" (1 Corinthians 3:16)

This notion that the community of believers, the body of Christ gathered for worship, is the primary subject of the liturgical action forms the basis for much of the teaching contained in the *Constitution on the Sacred Liturgy* of Vatican II. Aware that they needed to overcome centuries of Catholic piety that tended to involve the faithful as "strangers or silent spectators" (48), the bishops repeatedly insisted on the necessity of the "full, conscious, and active participation of all the faithful" in the liturgical action. (Cf. 11, 14, 19, 21, 30, 41, 48, etc.) After recognizing the various forms of Christ's presence in the liturgy (in the priest, in the eucharistic species, in the sacraments, in the word proclaimed), they added, "Lastly, he is present when the Church prays and sings, for he has promised 'where two or three are gathered together in my name there am I in the midst of them' (Matthew 18:20)." (7) When the Church gathers for prayer, it is Christ who prays!

The important symbolism involved in the action of God's people assembling for worship can be traced back into the earliest days of Jewish history. The act of gathering, in a sense, constitutes the people as God's chosen community. The "assembly" became historically a theological notion of real importance. Christian understandings of the role of the Holy Spirit in constituting God's people as a "holy temple" have deepened our appreciation for the role and dignity of the entire community of the faithful. When the church gathers, "there am I," promises the Lord.

We still have a great ways to go in heightening the appreciation of our Catholic faithful in this regard. The rush of families not to be "late for Mass," the search for a parking space in the crowded lot, the individualism and privatism that American culture associates with religious practice; such realities make it exceedingly difficult to develop an awareness of the sacramentality of the community itself as it gathers for worship. Yet these challenges must be met with heightened efforts if we are to instill in the young a strong appreciation for the important sacramental role that the assembly itself plays in the liturgy. Children need to be given a respect and even a reverence for the body of Christ that gathers in such rich diversity at every Sunday Eucharist. They should be helped to marvel at the awesome spectacle of people old and young, rich and poor, healthy and enfeebled, all coming together to proclaim the unity they share in Christ, "For in one Spirit we were all baptized into one body, whether Jews or Greek, slaves or free persons, and we were all given to drink of the one Spirit." (1 Corinthians 12:13) A number of our liturgical rituals where incense is used call for the assembly itself to be incensed as a sign of respect and reverence for the body of Christ. A commentary that accompanies the rites for dedicating a church captures wonderfully the essence of what one would want a child to grasp: "The incensation of the nave of the church indicates that the dedication makes it a house of prayer, but the people of God are incensed first, *because they are the living temple in which each faithful member is a spiritual altar.*" (16)

The Altar

The most important furnishing in a church is the altar, a fact that is almost always immediately clear from the visual and spatial arrangement of the space. The altar is a richly symbolic object, and children need to learn about its significance and the role it plays in celebrating the core mysteries of our salvation. As is so often true of our most important religious symbols, the altar evokes multiple traditions that have met in the person of Jesus.

The first tradition is that of the fellowship meal, which was so central to the ministry of Jesus. The Gospels are filled with stories of how Jesus ate with sinners as well as the righteous, the rich as well as the poor, the outcast of society as well as the elite of his day. It is no exaggeration to say that, in the ministry of Jesus, the "table" became perhaps the single most highly charged expression of the Good News of God's unconditional love. The Jewish scriptures had already by Jesus' time made the meal a symbol of divine blessings. He took that tradition to a new level by linking his own offer of table-fellowship with an invitation to participate in the reign of God. At the Last Supper, in the context of the Jewish passover meal, he connected the gift of his own body and blood, offered on the cross, to the new covenant. That new covenant in his blood was to be celebrated in a meal shared forevermore "in memory" of him. The disciples of Jesus were commanded to "do this," to take, bless, break, and share as a way of keeping alive not just his memory, but his living presence, in their midst.

Hence the altar, seen as a table on which the Lord's supper is celebrated, is a primary symbol meant to evoke the entire meaning of the life and ministry of the Lord. Children need to recognize the altar as a table, something that is not always obvious because of the way that the form and decoration of altars has evolved over the centuries. Most children, however, can be helped to make the connection between the altar in their parish church and a richly decorated dining room table (one that they have seen at least in pictures, if not in their own home). The altar cloth can be explained as a table cloth, and the placement of flowers and candles for a festive meal should be a familiar enough custom to help further the association. Likewise, the sacred vessels that are used for communion can be related to familiar dining utensils that are part of a child's experience. In short, a child ought to be helped to see the altar as a table around which we gather to celebrate the Lord's supper in fulfillment of his command. And, once that primary symbolism of the meal is established in the child's mind, the Gospel stories of Jesus welcoming one and all to table with him will provide the "background" against which our contemporary celebration of eucharist can likewise be experienced as a call to fellowship with Jesus.

The second tradition that has met in the person of Jesus is the notion that the table around which we gather for a meal is also an altar of sacrifice. Jesus himself, of course, is the source of this linkage, as the Gospels clearly show in the words of Institution at the last supper. But this is an association that is more difficult for children to make, since altars of sacrifice are not part of their common experience. The metaphorical language of our theological tradition that makes both the Lord's table and his cross into an altar of sacrifice is not something that children will spontaneously grasp.

That is why children will need to be familiar with the biblical stories in which the notion of sacrificial altars plays an important part. The custom of animal sacrifice—and even the Jewish rejection of human sacrifice (in the story of Abraham and Isaac)—is something that a child needs to learn about both through bible stories and through explanations of "how it was done" in ancient times. The idea that we return to God a portion of our blessings by "giving them up" is not too complex a notion for a child to grasp. How ancient religions "gave up" things to God through animal and cereal offerings usually fascinates youngsters. It is also helpful to explain that ancient peoples often believed that by eating a portion of what was offered to the gods, one could enter into a kind of "communion" with the divine that allowed one to share in the life-force of the divinity itself.

Once children have grasped these basic notions, it is possible for them to make sense out of our language that the altar is a table of sacrifice, where we offer to God the most precious gift of all, Jesus who died for our sins. Children are remarkably comfortable with the play of metaphor, and they can readily appreciate language that speaks of how we can and should place on the altar our own lives, offering them to God in union with Jesus, giving ourselves in love just as Jesus did, for the life of the world. In this regard it is helpful also to explain to children the origin of the custom of embedding a relic of one of the saints in an altar. Initially, altars (and the churches that housed them) were placed directly over the place where a martyr was buried. The sacrifice of one's life that martyrdom represents was celebrated at the altar of sacrifice, where Christ's sacrifice was presented to God in union with our own self-offering and that of the martyr. Today, in place of actually placing the altar over a martyr's grave, we place a relic of one of the saints within the altar on which the sacrifice is offered.

The centrality of the altar in our Catholic tradition is evident from the rubrics that require the ministers of the liturgy to reverence it with a bow and/or a ritual kiss. The altar is also incensed as a sign of reverence. Because it is linked so intimately to Christ's eucharistic presence as sacrament and sacrifice, the altar itself functions as a kind of symbol of the Lord in our midst. The *Catechism of the Catholic Church* quotes St. Ambrose who says, "For what is the altar of Christ if not the image of the body of Christ?" And elsewhere, "The altar represents the body [of Christ] and the body of Christ is on the altar." (1383) For this reason, we reverence the altar as a sign of Christ himself. Just as we teach children to genuflect before the blessed Sacrament, so also it is appropriate (in churches where the blessed Sacrament is reserved in a separate chapel) to teach them to reverence the altar with a bow as they enter the worship space.

The Ambo and the Books of Sacred Scripture

The term *ambo* is a Greek word for the raised platform from which the Scriptures are read. Historically, the ambo would usually have a reading desk on it, upon which rested the book of the Scriptures. In contemporary liturgical usage, the word *ambo* is used to refer both to the place and to the lectern from which the Scriptures are proclaimed.

It was St. Augustine who, referring to the two parts of the Mass (Liturgy of the Word, Liturgy of the Eucharist), first made reference to the two "tables" from which we are nourished—the table of the word and the table of Christ's body. For this reason, liturgical documents encourage the design of the ambo to reflect the "harmonious and close" relationship that exists between the altar and the ambo. (*Introduction to the Lectionary*, 32) Children should be given a sense that the ambo is, in its own way, as deserving of respect as is the altar, since from it God nourishes and enlightens our faith. One way that liturgical directives signal this importance is to restrict the use of the ambo, reserving it for the proclamation of Scripture, the Easter Exsultet, the homily, and the Prayer of the Faithful. It is not to be used by commentators, song leaders, or those making announcements.

Some churches have the custom of enthroning the book of God's word, either at the ambo or in another suitable place. Children will know, of course, that the book of God's word is called the Bible. They will usually not be aware that our liturgical tradition excerpts selected parts of the Bible and puts those texts together in separate volumes for use in our public worship. As they grow older, in the interest of their being more liturgically literate, it is good to explain to them the different ways that books containing parts of the Bible are used in the liturgy.

The Lectionary is the generic name for the volume that contains all of the readings that have been selected for use in our liturgical rituals. Current publishing practice has separated the Lectionary into one book for use on Sundays and major feasts, another for use on weekdays and to accompany other sacramental celebrations. There is also a Children's Lectionary that has been approved for use in Masses with Children. Since our Sunday readings are spread out over a three-year cycle, sometimes the Sunday Lectionary is printed as separate volumes for years A, B, and C.

In addition to the Lectionary that contains all of the readings (Old Testament, Psalm, New Testament, Gospel), publishers have been encouraged to follow the ancient tradition of producing a separate Book of the Gospels. The proclamation of the Gospel has always been regarded as the high point of the Liturgy of the Word, and so richly decorated books containing only the Gospel texts have long been in use. Today, more and more parish churches are using a separate Book of the Gospels, and it is helpful for children to recognize this distinction. Theoretically, yet another volume could be published containing the psalmody and other chants that are used in the liturgy. However, that seems to not be feasible given the many different musical settings in use today, and so it seems unlikely that children will need to be aware of any such collection used by the cantor.

While a knowledge of these many different ways of arranging the Scriptures for liturgical use might seem to border on liturgical trivia, there is a deeper issue at stake that is terribly significant. Children need to develop a keen sense of reverence that God continues to speak to his people in the Liturgy of the Word. Learning to respond, "Thanks be to God" and "Glory to you, Lord" can be a way that a child internalizes a fundamental attitude of openness to and thanksgiving for God's word in our lives. Similarly, introducing children to the little gesture of signing forehead, lips, and breast prior to the proclamation of the Gospel can be a moment of important catechesis on the respect we must pay to God's word. When children observe the Gospel procession on Sunday or on special feasts, complete with lit candles, incense and jubilant "Alleluia's," we need to make certain that they understand the reason for such prominence being given to what is being proclaimed. The Good News (Gospel) of our salvation is made present and real, alive and active, each and every time the Church at prayer proclaims the words of Jesus from one of the Gospel texts. No wonder that our response is "Praise to *you*, Lord Jesus Christ!"

Children are not expected to read the *Dogmatic Constitution on Divine Revelation, Dei Verbum*, promulgated at the Second Vatican Council. But they can grasp its most essential content by learning how to "read" what is conveyed in sign and symbol at each and every Sunday celebration, as God's people gather and listen attentively to the Liturgy of the Word. The profound truth that God has chosen to speak to us words of love, inviting on our part a response of faith—that truth is precisely what the young can be taught as they learn to understand what the ambo and the books of God's word are all about. Children will not need to read Vatican II's *Decree on the Pastoral Office of Bishops* nor the *Decree on the Ministry and Life of Priests* to know that the first task of the ordained is the ministry of the word, to preach and to teach authoritatively in the name of Jesus. As they experience the ambo as a true "table" from which they are fed, and the sacred books of Scripture as truly a "lamp" lighting their way, all that they need to know about the deposit of faith being contained in sacred Scripture and Tradition will have already been planted in their very bones.

The Baptismal Font and the Ambry

Theologians and church commentators who discuss the significance of the Second Vatican Council are in agreement that among its most important accomplishments was the renewed emphasis it placed on baptism as the foundational sacrament of the Christian life. This is a truth that we are only at the very earliest stages of appreciating. Centuries of neglect of a baptismal spirituality, as well as an exaggerated emphasis on the importance of Holy Orders, have had the practical effect of minimizing in people's minds the true significance of their baptism. One can test one's own sense of this by asking, "Which would feel like the greater honor: being elected pope or being baptized?" Theoretically, of course, we know that baptism is more important; but at a gut level, most would probably be inclined to pick the papacy as the greater honor.

The task of instilling in the next generation a proper perspective on the importance of baptism is a challenging one indeed. If the truth be told, we can almost always tell what is most important to someone by looking at where they invest their resources. The man who lives in a tumble-down shack, but has two or three flashy automobiles sitting in his driveway, would have a difficult time convincing me that he really does value a home for his family more than his own enchantment with sports cars. The history of church architecture reveals in much the same way the shifting priorities that have dominated Christian consciousness, and the progressive decline in our appreciation for the importance of baptism.

Our current liturgical theology would say that the three most prominent and distinguishing features of a Catholic church should be the altar, the ambo, and the baptismal font. But except for some surviving churches built in the fourth century and the centuries immediately thereafter, this balance seems totally absent in most Catholic places of worship. There are, certainly, exceptions to be found in a few very recently constructed edifices. However, the architecture of most parish churches reflects our centuries of neglect of the significance of baptism. The subliminal message that is given to children when the baptismal font is a tawdry little bowl, stuck in a remote corner of the church, is difficult to overcome. Communities with impressive fonts, prominently placed, and clearly valued and prized as objects of importance, will find it much, much easier to help children appreciate the importance of baptism. Nonetheless, parents and educators have a duty to introduce children to the notion that the place of baptism is one of the most important places in the church building.

The proliferation of holy water fonts and the custom of blessing oneself with holy water upon entering the church is a surviving link with an ancient theology of baptism that prized the waters of rebirth, and sought to renew an appreciation for the sacrament every time a Christian entered the church. Children should be told of the link between the baptismal font and those tiny holy water dishes. They should be encouraged to remember that each time they bless themselves with holy water in the name of the Trinity, what they are really doing is repeating their baptismal profession of faith. The rite of blessing and sprinkling water that is sometimes used on Sunday mornings is a welcome addition to our eucharistic ritual that makes those connections explicit.

It is worthwhile to examine carefully the decorative details that are part of the parish's baptismal font. Even when the font is artistically inferior and of a size or placement that bespeaks profound neglect, there are usually iconographic details that can be used to explain the theology of baptism. Children love to explore and investigate for clues to a puzzle. The identification and interpretation of the baptismal font's iconography can be a rich and rewarding opportunity to discuss with a child what baptism is all about and why it is so important.

An even more fascinating project would be to obtain a book depicting ancient baptistries and baptismal fonts, and to explore the rich theology of baptism that is embodied in the incredibly lush artistry with which many of those ancient baptismal places were adorned. Fonts that were octagonal in shape evoked the eschatological "eighth day"; those that were tomb-like hearkened back to Paul's understanding in Romans, chapter six, of baptism as death with Christ; while womb-like shapes spoke of baptismal rebirth and the theology of John 3, where Jesus speaks to Nicodemus about being born again of water and Spirit. There are depictions of paradise, with the fabulous waters of Ezekiel's vision in chapter 47 that transform the desert into a place of refreshment. The images tumble over one another: Noah in the waters of the flood, Moses at the Red Sea, Jesus in the Jordan River, the Spirit hovering over the waters of creation, the blood and water flowing from the side of Christ on the cross. It is probably fair to say that the iconography of baptism is as abundant and detailed as that of any single area of Christian theology. What a wonderful opportunity such images present for sharing with a child our Christian belief in baptism as the foundational sacrament!

An important element of church architecture associated with baptism is the ambry, the repository for the sacred oils. In many new churches the oils are kept in a location that is prominently placed in relation to the baptismal font. The majority of older churches, however, most likely have a cupboard-like door on the sanctuary wall or in the sacristy with the words *Olea Sacra* (Holy Oils) inscribed on it. Children should know that there are three oils that the Church uses in its liturgical rituals. The most important of these is chrism, a richly perfumed olive oil that is used in baptism, confirmation, and holy orders, as well as for several other rites (e.g., the consecration of an altar). The second oil, also associated with Christian initiation, is the oil of catechumens, which is administered to adults during the period of the catechumenate prior to their baptism (infants may be anointed with this oil during the actual ceremony of their baptism). And, finally, the oil of the sick is used for the sacrament of the Anointing of the Sick.

The historical significance attached to anointing is complex. Both Scripture and Christian tradition have contributed to the diverse layers of meaning associated with sacred oil. In the Jewish scriptures there are references to the anointing of priests, prophets, and kings. These anointings seem to be associated with consecration to God and a strengthening for one's mission. Christian tradition also features prominently the healing and exorcistic associations of anointing with oil. As with so many of our sacramental symbols, it would be a mistake to try to narrow the significance of oil or its use in a given anointing to a single meaning. Rather, the richness of a symbol's meaning is indicative of the multifaceted experience of grace that characterizes all of our encounters with God. Children usually grasp this intuitively, unencumbered as they are by our adult need to define and distinguish. Children can usually grasp the significance of our sacred oils very easily if they are reminded of how a mother puts on perfume for special occasions, or what it feels like to have lotion applied to sunburn, or ointment on an aching muscle.

The Tabernacle

It would probably surprise most Catholics to know that for the first millennium of the Christian era, there were no tabernacles in churches that allowed believers to "stop by and make a visit to the blessed Sacrament." Devotion to the blessed Sacrament reserved in the tabernacle is a development of the second millennium. However, from the earliest times, it was the custom to preserve some of the eucharist after the celebration so that it could be taken to the sick, and especially to the dying. That ancient tradition is still described in the liturgical documents as the primary reason for the practice of reservation, although today reservation to foster devotion is also acknowledged as an important aspect of Catholic piety.

The place of reservation for the blessed Sacrament has seen considerable variety over the centuries. What was initially a private practice developed into many different ways of keeping the eucharist, either in a side sacristy or within the main body of the church. The blessed Sacrament was sometimes suspended in a container over the altar, or placed in a eucharistic tower on a pillar, or in a niche in the wall. The container we call a tabernacle today has been the almost exclusive receptacle for eucharistic reservation since the Council of Trent. Recent liturgical legislation encourages the practice of a separate chapel where the tabernacle is placed and private devotion encouraged, but flexibility is permitted in view of the many different architectural arrangements of existing churches. The custom of signaling the presence of the blessed Sacrament by a burning candle in a "sanctuary lamp" (usually of red glass, but not always) is still maintained.

Devotion to Christ in the blessed Sacrament is a wonderfully rich prayer experience that children should be introduced to at an early age. The development of a personal relationship with Jesus through awareness of his real presence in the eucharist contributes to the growth of an affective spirituality that is extremely important for children. One can avoid the pitfall of approaching the blessed Sacrament as if it were a static object by stressing for children the dynamic nature of Christ's personal presence in the eucharist. This happens naturally when we link the reserved sacrament to its origin in the celebration of the Mass, where the assembly both *receives* and *becomes* the body of Christ by encountering him in Word and Sacrament. Children should be taught the significance of a genuflection, which is both a profession of faith and a sign of respect for Christ sacramentally present in the tabernacle.

We also help children to develop a healthy devotion to the Blessed Sacrament by reminding them to hold in prayer those for whom the eucharist is reserved in the first place: the sick whose sufferings link them to the passion of Christ in a uniquely powerful way. The habit of prayer before the blessed Sacrament is a unitive experience, through which an individual gradually grows in openness to Christ and to all who are "in Christ." Sunday Mass always ends with a dismissal that sends us into the world to bring God's Good News to those who suffer. So, too, healthy devotion to the reserved eucharist results in a deepening solidarity with the Christ whom we recognize in our suffering brothers and sisters (Matthew 25).

The Reconciliation Chapel/Confessional

Children who are preparing for their First Reconciliation should routinely be introduced to the places where the Sacrament of Penance is ordinarily celebrated. In most parishes, this will include both a Reconciliation Chapel and a confessional. In order to insure that they are comfortable with how these spaces work, children should be given a "guided tour" and allowed to ask any questions they might have. There ought to be no mystery about these settings, and so it is important to allow the children to inspect the area where the priest sits as well as the penitent's space. Where a two-sided confessional is still in use, particular attention should be paid to helping the youngsters understand how the sliding windows and any system of signal lights work. In the case of a Reconciliation Chapel, they should be shown that the option of an anonymous confession is available, as well as a face-to-face encounter with the priest.

In addition to these "logistical" introductions, it is important to offer children a perspective on the Sacrament of Penance that is reassuring and inviting. Knowledge that anonymity is available is a concern for some children; for all, it is important to discuss the nature of the "seal" of confession, which strictly forbids the priest from divulging any aspect of what a penitent tells him. Beyond these reassurances, what is most critical is that children perceive the Sacrament of Penance as an experience of the healing and forgiving love of Jesus himself. The priest stands in the place of Christ the Good Shepherd, whose sole concern is to restore the lost sheep to the safety of the flock. Some children have problems with forgiveness, either accepting it, trusting that it is real, or offering it themselves. These difficulties are usually rooted in life experiences that have been problematic. Whenever such difficulties are discovered, children should be offered images of the unconditional love of God that Jesus proclaimed. Gospel stories such as the parable of the prodigal son or the tale of Jesus and the tax collector can help even the most reticent child to understand that the Sacrament of Penance is about God's forgiveness, not divine wrath or judgement. An adult who has a child's trust is in a unique position to communicate a positive attitude toward this sacrament that many find difficult. Sharing one's own personal experience of joy in receiving God's forgiveness at the hands of a priest—leading by example—is generally the most effective way of doing this.

Robert D. Duggan

The Crucifix/Cross and
the Stations of the Cross

It would be hard to find a religious symbol more central to our faith than the cross. A typical church often has many different expressions of this most important sign of our faith. Most often, there is a large crucifix or cross directly behind or above the altar. It is unfortunate that in some people's minds the crucifix is seen as a Catholic symbol, while the cross without a corpus is considered Protestant. Nothing could be further from the truth! In fact, Catholicism has rich and ancient traditions of both kinds of renderings of the Lord's passion. Historically, the portrayal of a simple wooden cross without a body seems to be more ancient. But aesthetic considerations and shifting popular piety have in the course of time placed on the cross figures of Jesus' body, most often with a realism that displays the sufferings of his passion, but sometimes displaying a glorified Christ or a Christ in priestly garb who reigns from the cross as from a throne. While different portrayals certainly highlight different aspects of our faith in Christ, one ought not to make negative, *a priori* judgements about any given option.

Children are open to a variety of ways to experience the symbol of the cross, and they should be encouraged to explore what any given representation evokes in them. As a religious symbol, the crucifix/cross is always an invitation to enter more deeply into the mystery which it represents. For example, the cross that is carried in processions of all sorts is itself a provocative statement of the nature of Christian discipleship. Jesus clearly tells his disciples that they must "follow" in his footsteps as he makes his way to his destiny in Jerusalem. (Cf. Mark 10:32ff) Those who walk in procession behind the cross of Jesus are proclaiming with their very bodies that they accept this aspect of discipleship.

The Stations of the Cross offer a good example of how popular devotion has resulted in a highly developed spiritual sensitivity to the story of Jesus' passion. The origins of the stations go back to pilgrimages to the holy places in Jerusalem, where pilgrims commemorated the journey of Jesus to Calvary by retracing his actual footsteps. As we now pray them, the stations are meant to foster in us an awareness of Jesus' passion, so that we will experience greater solidarity with him and with all whose sufferings are represented by his cross. This devotion is meant to be prayed by walking from station to station. The practice of only the priest or a few ministers walking around the church, while others watch, is not the ideal and should only be done out of necessity. When each station contains a visual representation of the scene that is held up for reflection, we have a wonderful opportunity to engage the imagination of children. If they are not already familiar with the scriptural story behind the stations, children should be introduced to each of the stations by sharing with them an evocative narrative that highlights how much the Lord loved us to suffer for us in that way. Their prayer response to that narrative, hopefully, will include intercession for those who suffer today from analogous tortures of mind and body.

Devotional Areas

One of the distinguishing features of Catholic churches has long been the many evidences that they contain of a rich devotional life on the part of the faithful. At times the fervor of piety was such that it resulted in an excessive emphasis on the devotional to the neglect of the liturgy itself; and, at times, great piety seemed to generate a great deal of bad art. But at its root, our Catholic love for the saints is a wonderful expression of the important role that the Communion of Saints plays in our understanding of the Church.

Children easily identify with the images of Mary and the other saints that populate niches and corners and pedestals throughout our churches. Adults should encourage in children a healthy devotion to these ancestors in the Faith who serve as role models for young and old alike. Whether or not your parish church has flickering votive lights that fascinate and attract, there are surely statues and other artistic portrayals that will engage youthful imaginations and depict the human side of our Church. These portrayals offer an excellent opportunity to discuss with children the Communion of Saints, the teaching that the Church embraces in a single family all who have lived and died in the Lord. One rarely hears these days about the Church militant, suffering and triumphant, but each and every devotion to one of the saints holds open the possibility of a "teachable moment" for impressionable young minds looking for heroes to emulate. The Christmas crèche is a wonderful chance to share with children the story of our salvation in a way that is easily accessible to them and that will make deep and lasting impressions.

Vestments

The special clothing that ministers of the liturgy wear is a source of real fascination for children. One could explore a great deal of trivia when it comes to the field of ecclesiastical garb, but there are a few basics that are quite important for children to know. First of all, the full-length white garment, called an alb, worn by the priest and sometimes by other ministers is in actuality the basic liturgical garment of every Christian. It is, in fact, none other than the robe that is given to every Christian at baptism. Far from being a sign of ecclesial office, the alb is the "birthright" of all the baptized. Our association of this garment with only priests or other official ministers is understandable. Nonetheless, children ought to be told that the little white robe in which they were baptized was in fact a mini alb!

It is the stole which a deacon, priest, or bishop wears when celebrating the liturgy that is the "official" garment designating his status in ordained ministry. Other clothing that he wears in addition will vary depending on the rite involved. For example, the priest will wear a chasuble for Eucharist, or a cope (a cape-like garment) for processions or Benediction of the Blessed Sacrament. The black cassock that a priest or altar server sometimes wears has no official liturgical standing. The surplice (the shorter white garment worn over a cassock) is simply an abbreviated alb, and again has no official liturgical standing. Similarly, choir robes or other garments that are sometimes worn by various liturgical ministers are arbitrary garments that do not have any formal place in the repertoire of liturgical vesture.

Children are keen to notice the variations in color that are reflected in liturgical garments and decorations. It is helpful if they can learn the "code" of each of the liturgical colors. White and gold are used for festive occasions, such as Easter and Christmas, as well as the liturgies of Christian initiation and Christian burial. Green designates Ordinary Time. Shades of violet or purple signal Advent and Lent. (More and more communities are finding it helpful to distinguish these two seasons by a more bluish purple in Advent.) Rose is still permitted on Gaudete Sunday in Advent and Laetare Sunday in Lent. (These names stem from the first word in Latin of the entrance song for the respective Sundays.) Red is associated with feasts of the Holy Spirit and martyrs, while black is still permitted for funerals (although white seems more and more the preferred choice in our culture).

The Books We Use at Liturgy

Children notice that in our life of worship we use many different books. Depending on their age and interest, children should be familiarized with what all of those different books are about. We have already mentioned above the most important book we use, the book of God's Word, which our liturgical tradition has excerpted as a Lectionary. In the official jargon of the Roman liturgy, the Lectionary is only half of a larger "book," called the Roman Missal. The other "half" of the Missal is published separately as the Sacramentary, and that volume contains all of the prayers that the priest needs for the Eucharist. The Lectionary and the Sacramentary, then, are the two official volumes routinely needed for the celebration of Sunday Mass.

There is another liturgical "book," which does not exist as a separate volume, called the Roman Ritual. The Ritual theoretically contains all of the other sacramental rites of the Church, but those rites are usually published in individual volumes (for baptism, confirmation, and so forth). The final book that a parish church regularly uses is the Book of Blessings, which contains official prayers of blessing for a wide variety of people, objects, and occasions. The Roman liturgical library also includes two books that are for use by a bishop. The first, the Pontifical, contains the actual prayers of the various rites presided over by a bishop. The second, called the Ceremonial, contains the directions about how to prepare for and execute ceremonies involving a bishop.

In addition to these official liturgical books, parishes routinely provide members of the assembly with a variety of printed resources to assist them in participating fully in the Sunday Eucharist. There are hymnals, seasonal missalettes, and sometimes weekly worship guides that encourage people to join fully in the celebration. It is important to spend time with children to make sure that they are familiar with and comfortable using these resources to the best of their ability. Children need to feel included, and allowing them access to the resources which the rest of the community uses is a major way to do that. Some communities offer leaflets and other materials designed specifically for children. While there can be a certain benefit to such materials, it is important that these not distract from or substitute for a child's active participation in the liturgical action. It is far better for children to be engaged actively in following the liturgy to the extent they can, rather than to have their heads buried in a children's booklet, coloring pictures of Jesus, and oblivious to the liturgy itself. Some prayer books that are aimed at children make the same mistake of so engaging children in the pages of the prayer book that they do not attend to the liturgy itself. Parents will need to keep a careful eye out to determine how best to use printed materials so that children will meet the aim of the liturgical renewal of Vatican II, i.e., "full, conscious, and active participation" in the liturgy.

2

SACRED TIME

The Notion of Sacred Time

Children raised in our technological society find it quite challenging to think of time as anything more than a scientific measurement. Accustomed to the flashing numbers on their digital watches, many youngsters have even lost a sense of the graceful passage of time that comes from watching the sweep of the hands on a clock. The impatience with waiting that is so prominent a part of our culture of instant gratification makes it even more difficult for children to experience the passage of time as anything more than a relentless tedium.

Parents and teachers who seek to introduce children of the Digital Age to the notion that time itself can be experienced as sacred—something to be cherished rather than "gotten over with" as quickly as possible—are faced with a formidable task. Yet, an appreciation for time as sacred is a fundamental perspective of our Judeo-Christian tradition of faith, and one that we must not fail to instill in the young. In his Apostolic Letter, *On Keeping the Lord's Day Holy* (*Dies Domini*), Pope John Paul II has written, "In Christianity time has a fundamental importance. Within the dimension of time the world was created; within it the history of salvation unfolds, finding its culmination in the 'fullness of time' of the Incarnation, and its goal in the glorious return of the Son of God at the end of time. In Jesus Christ, the Word made flesh, time becomes a dimension of God, who is himself eternal". (74) Since both creation and redemption happen within time, time itself becomes part of the unfolding mystery of God's love for us.

The attitude toward time that is found in the biblical writings is in many ways much more sophisticated than the one-dimensional approach of our technological age. In fact, the bible uses two different words to designate two quite distinct understandings of time. The first word (in Greek, *chronos*) is the root of our English word "chronological" and refers to the measured passage of time. This kind of time is a commodity, a unit of measure, oblivious to the meaning of the events that transpire within its inexorable passage. The ancients knew well the workings of *chronos*. They were not at all oblivious to this secular, scientific understanding of time that is so pervasive in our contemporary culture.

But they also knew time as *kairos*, as a sacred moment, a fullness in which one day is as a thousand years or, as the psalmist puts it, "A thousand years in [God's] eyes are merely a yesterday." (Psalm 90:4) The word *kairos* describes an experience of time that is without measure, time that one experiences as so full of the divine presence that it makes chronological measurement meaningless. "Better one day in your courts than a thousand elsewhere," the psalmist writes (Psalm 84:11), capturing perfectly the sense that *kairos* is to be cherished and celebrated, not hoarded, measured, or wasted. Sacred time is the Lord's time, a timeless time, a moment apart from the relentless, inexorable passage that brings death and despair. In sacred time, God works miracles of grace. This is the sense of time that St. Paul refers to in describing the mystery of the Incarnation: "But when the fullness of time had come, God sent his Son, born of a woman, . . . so that we might receive adoption." (Galatians 4:4-5) This kind of time is always about the grace of salvation that is offered to us, an invitation that we can receive only if we are willing to leave *chronos* and enter God's *kairos*.

The decision to leave *chronos* and enter *kairos* is a choice that we are free to make or not. Christian faith asserts that in the new dispensation, the fullness of God's grace is now available to us, always and everywhere. Mark's Gospel sums up the core of our belief in this regard when he quotes the very first words of Jesus' preaching: "This is the time of fulfillment. The kingdom of God is at hand." (Mark 1:15) But however much we would wish to be constantly aware of this "time of fulfillment," God's *kairos*, we know the reality of our human lives, and how often and easily we are drawn back into *chronos*. It is because of this inevitable "slippage" into mere *chronos* that we have learned the importance of sacred ritual. For, it is one of the primary characteristics of religious ritual is that it is time set apart, sacred time, in which we have access to the "timeless" experience of God's presence.

One of the functions of our sacred liturgy, then, is to allow us to become more easily aware of and open ourselves up to God's grace. It does this by inviting us to and supporting us as we experience *kairos*, a time that is sacred because it is filled with the fullness of God. All of this may sound terribly theological and complex. But, in reality, each of us has many first-hand, ordinary experiences of what the biblical writers called *kairos*. Whenever we allow ourselves to "get lost" in the wonder of a sunset, to lose track of time gazing at a beautiful mountain range or the loveliness of a single flower, we have entered *kairos*. New Age gurus who train people in breathing or other relaxation techniques are really just introducing busy folks to some simple disciplines that allow them to put aside *chronos* for a brief respite. A lazy summer afternoon at the beach can be an exquisite experience of *kairos*; so, too, is the time between lovers usually just such a "timeless" moment.

What our tradition of Christian liturgy does is make the religious dimension of such experiences explicit. In the framework of the Church's liturgy, there is a focused and deliberate attempt to "re-claim" all of time as God's time. By an intentional effort to structure all of time within the context of the Christian mystery, the Church invites us to experience every part of every day as a "graced" moment of *kairos*. In the sections that follow, we will explore the major outlines of how the Church attempts to "redeem" time itself as sacred in the course of the liturgical cycle.

Before we move on to those considerations, however, it may be helpful to comment on how important it is that children be prepared for and introduced to an experience of sacred time. As we indicated above, our culture does very little to develop in children an appreciation for *kairos*, either in its secular or sacred forms. Social commentators, childhood development specialists, and educators are unanimous in their observations about how frequently today's children are subject to stresses that make their life far too pressured and rushed. We need to be deliberate and persistent in our efforts to help children learn the art of spending time timelessly. The ability to engage in contemplation is really what is at issue here. For children whose internal rhythms are in hyper-drive due to the speed of computer games or the rapid fire images they watch on TV, slowing down their internal rhythms will not come easily. Children need to practice the disciplines involved in an awareness that is focused without being forced.

Children thrive on ritual, of course. One of the bedtime rituals I have observed in the children of some close friends is surely typical of many families. It involves a pattern of "quieting down" that includes putting on pajamas, reading a set number of favorite stories, being tucked into bed, and then saying prayers about the events of the day and the children's loved ones. What I witness in this predictable ritual is how readily the familiar ritual helps the children slip into a frame of mind that prepares them for a relaxed sleep. I have also seen the same mother sit quietly in a rocking chair with her toddler, talking softly as she encourages the little one to observe the birds coming and going to the birdbath in the back yard. The child loses track of time and learns to enjoy the beauty of just "being," enfolded in the arms of an unconditional love. Whether she knows it or not, that young mother is showing her children how to experience *kairos*, how to let go of busy activity and allow contemplative awareness to develop naturally. One can only hope that when her children participate in formal schooling, their teachers will continue that same training, building into the classroom routine regular experiences that will further develop—and name in explicitly religious fashion—the art of contemplative prayer. When such is the case, children are much more open to what the liturgy attempts to do with its rituals that "re-claim" time as sacred.

Sunday: the Lord's Day

The original Christian feast day is Sunday, the Lord's Day, on which we celebrate his resurrection from the dead. Since the very beginning, disciples of Jesus have gathered on a particular day of the week, in obedience to his command to "do this" in his memory. Dom Gregory Dix, the great British liturgist, asked, "Was ever another command so obeyed?" In a famous passage from his study of the Mass, Dix marvels at "those innumerable millions of entirely obscure faithful men and women" over the centuries who have kept holy the Lord's Day, in fulfillment of his command. "Every one with his or her own individual hopes and fears and joys and sorrows and loves—and sins and temptations and prayers. . . . They have left no slightest trace in this world, not even a name, but have passed to God utterly forgotten by men. Yet each of them once believed and prayed as I believe and pray, and found it hard and grew slack and sinned and repented and fell again. Each of them worshiped at the Eucharist and found their thoughts wandering and tried again. . ." It is hard to overstate the significance of this marvelous continuity of experience that stretches back in unbroken fashion over two millennia. When we gather on Sunday to celebrate the Eucharist, we are doing something very venerable, we are fulfilling a destiny as ancient as the Church itself.

On the feast of Pentecost in 1998, Pope John Paul II issued an Apostolic Letter, *On Keeping the Lord's Day Holy*, in which he described the importance of this day of days. A list of the chapter headings of that letter and a partial indication of some of the topics covered indicates just how important Sunday is in Christian tradition.

Robert D. Duggan

Chapter 1 - The Day of the Lord
  • Celebration of the creator's work
  • Shabbat: The creator's joyful rest
Chapter 2 - The Day of Christ
  • Day of the Risen Christ and of
    the Gift of the Holy Spirit
  • The weekly Easter
  • The day of the new creation
Chapter 3 - The Day of the Church
  • The Eucharistic Assembly: Heart of Sunday
  • From Mass to Mission
Chapter 4 - The Day of Man
  • Sunday: Day of joy, rest, and solidarity
Chapter 5 - The Day of Days
  • Sunday, the primordial feast, revealing the
    meaning of time
  • Christ the Alpha and Omega of time
  • Sunday in the liturgical year

As the Holy Father's letter indicates, our tradition of Sunday is rooted in the Jewish theology of creation, and its affirmation of the goodness of all that God has made. Likewise, the Christian Sunday has assimilated the Jewish notion of Sabbath as a time to celebrate that goodness by joining in the creator's rest. The challenge we face trying to recapture the idea of Sunday as a day of rest and re-creation is enormous in today's world of Sunday shopping and children's organized sports and other activities.

In chapter 2, the Holy Father explains that Sunday receives its specific character from its link with the day of the Lord's resurrection and his gift of the Spirit to the Church. Sunday is the Church's original celebration of the Paschal Mystery, which is why our liturgical tradition calls it the "weekly Easter." Long before there was an annual observance of Easter among Christians, Jesus' disciples were gathering faithfully every Sunday to commemorate the dying and rising of the Lord. Sunday was, for them, the "new creation," the eschatological "eighth day" on which all things had been made new by the gift of his Spirit.

The practice of gathering on Sunday to celebrate the Eucharist was seen as so important an aspect of Christian faith that the early believers did so even at the risk of their lives. To come together for the eucharist on Sunday was simply what a Christian did, regardless of the cost or effort involved. That is why the Holy Father quotes the words ascribed to the martyrs of Abitina, in Proconsular Africa during the persecution of the Emperor Diocletian, when Christian assemblies were banned with the greatest severity. Many were courageous enough to defy the imperial decree and accepted death rather than miss the Sunday Eucharist. The Holy Father says, "They replied to their accusers: 'Without fear of any kind we have celebrated the Lord's Supper, because it cannot be missed; that is our law'; 'We cannot live without the Lord's Supper.' As she confessed her faith, one of the martyrs said: 'Yes, I went to the assembly and I celebrated the Lord's Supper with my brothers and sisters, because I am a Christian.'" (*Dies Domini* 46) It is testimony such as this that children need to hear if they are to understand why there is still a Sunday obligation to participate in the Eucharist even in the third millennium!

The Holy Father also calls Sunday the "Day of the Church," because it is the day *par excellence* when the community assembles for worship and for fellowship. But Sunday is also about the mission of the Church, which is why from the earliest times the Eucharist has ended with the charge, *Ite, Missa est.* Go, the Mass is ended. Go forth, into the world, and bring the Good News of God's love to all peoples. Go! You are sent to proclaim a day of favor from the Lord, to carry on the mission and ministry of Jesus, to bring light to those in darkness and freedom to those imprisoned. From the beginning, the Sunday Eucharistic gathering was a launching pad for disciples who were sent to transform the world into the place of God's reign of peace and justice. Sunday, then, is to be a day of joyful celebration, of rest and renewal, as well as solidarity with the poor and the lowly. The Pope quotes a sermon from St. John Chrysostom, who told his listeners, "He who said: 'This is my body' is the same One who said: 'You saw me hungry and you gave me no food,' and 'Whatever you did to the least of my brothers you did also to me.' What good is it if the eucharistic table is overloaded with golden chalices, when he is dying of hunger? Start by satisfying his hunger, and then with what is left you may adorn the altar as well.'" (71) The Holy Father goes on to say, "Inviting to a meal people who are alone, visiting the sick, providing food for needy families, spending a few hours in voluntary work and acts of solidarity: These would certainly be ways of bringing into people's lives the love of Christ received at the Eucharistic table." (72) Families that take seriously the Pontiff's suggestions will teach their children by example the true meaning of Sunday as a day of solidarity.

In the final chapter of his Apostolic Letter, the Pope touches on how it is that Sunday reveals the ultimate meaning of all time. He says, "Springing from the Resurrection, [the Christian Sunday] cuts through human time, the months, the years, the centuries, like a directional arrow which points them towards their target: Christ's second coming. Sunday foreshadows the last day, the day of the Parousia, which in a way is already anticipated by Christ's glory in the event of the Resurrection." (75)

This magnificent vision of the Holy Father ought not to be considered too sophisticated to be grasped by children. In essence, it is as simple as helping them to understand the meaning of the Memorial Acclamation that we often use during the Eucharistic Prayer: "Christ has died, Christ is risen. Christ will come again." In his Apostolic Letter, the Pope recognizes the enormous pastoral challenge that we face in trying to restore Sunday to its rightful place of prominence in the Christian life. Parents and teachers who themselves have deepened their own appreciation for the stature that Sunday deserves will find it much easier to convey to the young a proper regard for this fundamental Christian feast.

Robert D. Duggan

The Liturgical Year

We mentioned above that the earliest Christian liturgical cycle was a weekly one, revolving around Sunday. However, the development of an annual cycle around the observance of Easter was not long in coming. The Gospels' linkage of the Christian Pasch (i.e., the dying and rising of Jesus) to the Jewish passover made it inevitable that an annual observance would be forthcoming. When, in fact, that annual commemoration first began, it was not preceded by the period of preparation we now know as Lent, nor followed by any extended celebration until Pentecost, the fiftieth day. But by the time the first millennium was half over, the basic outlines of the entire liturgical year as we know it today had developed, including the seasons of Lent, Easter, Advent, and Christmas. The development of an annual cycle celebrating the feasts of the saints, especially the martyrs, was also well underway by that time.

The liturgical reform agenda of the Second Vatican Council included the revision of the official Roman Calendar that sets out the structure of the annual liturgical cycle. That revised calendar was promulgated in 1969 and provides the basic framework of feasts and seasons through which the Church claims the entire year as sacred time. We suggested earlier that one might imagine a society in which none of the resources of modern catechesis are available. In such a society it was, in fact, the liturgical cycle of feasts and seasons celebrating the Christian mysteries that conveyed to young and old alike a basic understanding of our faith. The *Constitution on the*

Sacred Liturgy acknowledged this formative impact of the liturgical year. Referring to the annual cycle of liturgical celebrations, it observed, "In the course of the year, moreover, [the Church] unfolds the whole mystery of Christ . . ." (102)

Helping children to experience the liturgical cycle in such a way that they grasp "the whole mystery of Christ" is the task of their parents and teachers. That task is made significantly easier in parishes where the liturgy is celebrated lavishly and well. But even in communities still suffering the constraints of a liturgical minimalism, the potential impact of living deeply the rhythms of the liturgical calendar ought not to be underestimated. All of us live according to many different calendars. We live in a pluralistic society where many school districts observe calendars that include both secular holidays and the holy days of various world religions. There are other calendars that shape our attitudes and values as well. I refer, of course, to things like sports calendars (try scheduling *anything* on Super Bowl Sunday!), political calendars (that saturate the media with ad campaigns at various times), fiscal and tax-year calendars (that often influence our economic decisions), and so forth. It has been said that if you want to know what people's values *really* are, find out what calendars they live by.

The Church invites children to live by a particular calendar, a rhythm of feasts and seasons that not only marks out the times but also gives meaning and direction to our lives. Our annual liturgical cycle is a statement of faith put into the form of designated celebrations and periods of time that call for a particular focus and, often, for particular disciplines. The *Constitution on the Sacred Liturgy* says, "In the various seasons of the year and in keeping with her traditional discipline, the Church completes the formation of the faithful by means of pious practices for soul and body, by instruction, prayer, and works of penance and mercy." (105) It is incumbent on adults to understand thoroughly the renewed "shape" of our liturgical calendar so that they can pass on to the next generation a proper understanding of how we are meant to observe and celebrate "the whole mystery of Christ." The comments that follow are meant to help clarify the renewed liturgical vision that the revised calendar embodies.

The Paschal Triduum

The influence of our consumer culture on our children's attitudes and values is enormous. One would have to search a long, long time to discover a child for whom Christmas is not the most important feast day of the entire year. Nonetheless, our liturgical tradition takes a quite countercultural stand in its insistence that the Easter Triduum is "the culmination of the entire liturgical year." (*Roman Calendar* 18) Nothing, in fact, can compare in importance to the Triduum, which celebrates the core experience of salvation as we have come to know it in the dying and rising of Jesus. In the three major liturgies that constitute the Triduum, the very essence of our Christian faith is celebrated.

The Triduum ("three days") is not considered part of Lent, but is in fact the official beginning of the Pasch itself. It is reckoned according to the ancient method of calculating the beginning of a new liturgical day at sunset. Thus, the Triduum begins with the evening Mass of the Lord's supper on Holy Thursday, and continues until evening prayer on Easter Sunday. The Easter Vigil, celebrated during the darkness of Holy Saturday night, is the high point of the Triduum and the most solemn and sacred celebration of the entire liturgical year. It is a liturgy so rich, engaging, and formative of faith that one would wish every Catholic child could participate in it each and every year. Indeed, though not realistic, the ideal would be for every child—and adult—to participate in all three of the major celebrations of the Triduum (on Holy Thursday, Good Friday, and the Saturday Vigil). These three days should be thought of as if they were a single celebration, prolonged for three days, rather than three separate feast days.

One element of the renewal called for in the *Constitution on the Sacred Liturgy* has not received much notice and has not yet found its way to a significant degree into the lived experience of the Catholic people. The *Constitution* says, "The paschal fast must be kept sacred. It should be celebrated everywhere on Good Friday, and where possible should be prolonged throughout Holy Saturday so that the faithful may attain the joys of the Sunday of the resurrection with uplifted and responsive minds." (110) The revised Roman calendar that was subsequently issued indicated that following the completion of the liturgical service on Holy Thursday, the Church should enter into the paschal fast which "is observed everywhere." (*Roman Calendar* 20) This fast is distinct from the Lenten fast. Current legislation requires of adults only that they observe Good Friday as a day of fasting, but the spirit of the Triduum—and the most ancient practice of the Church—suggest the value and importance of observing the entire paschal fast. Children, of course, ought not to be burdened with too rigorous an experience of fasting. However, they ought to be introduced to this very meaningful ancient discipline and to its value as a discipline of solidarity with those who are preparing for baptism at the Vigil. As an increasing number of parishes focus attention on those in the catechumenate who will be initiated at the Vigil, the idea of fasting in solidarity with them makes more and more sense.

Some ethnic communities have preserved the custom of bringing food (in an Easter basket) to the parish church on Holy Saturday to be blessed. This custom is a remnant of earlier generations' observance of the Paschal fast, which was broken with great feasting following the celebration of the Vigil. When families today observe the Paschal fast only on Good Friday, the gathering for dinner on Easter Sunday afternoon lacks the impact of an Easter feast that follows immediately on a time of fasting. Families might want to rethink this situation and develop a new approach to the pattern of fasting-feasting in a way that will better capture the liturgical rhythm of the Triduum. Linking whatever family customs are adopted in this regard to the catechumens' experience of baptismal rebirth at the Vigil is a wonderful way to help children "make sense" out of our theology of Christ's resurrection and its connection to the sacraments of Christian initiation.

The Easter Season

The liturgical season of Easter begins with the Vigil and lasts for fifty days, concluding with Pentecost Sunday. The fifty days that comprise the Easter season "are celebrated as one feast day, sometimes called 'the great Sunday.'" (*Roman Calendar* 22) The first eight days, from Easter Sunday to the Second Sunday of Easter, are regarded as the Octave of Easter and are celebrated as solemnities of the Lord.

We are given an insight into the specific nature of this season by the *Rite of Christian Initiation of Adults*, which designates it as the Period of Post-baptismal Catechesis or Mystagogy. The Church prolongs its celebration of the Pasch by focusing during this time on its newly initiated members who, in their experience of rebirth by water and Spirit, become "living sacraments" of the presence of the risen one in our midst. The prayers and readings of the season are about some aspect of the mystery of Christian initiation, either focusing on what the sacraments do to the individual believer, or how they transform the entire community. It is a mistake to compartmentalize the meaning of Easter and Pentecost, suggesting that Easter is about Jesus' resurrection and Pentecost about the gift of the Holy Spirit. From the perspective of the liturgy, there is a single mystery, and the believer's encounter with the risen Christ is also an experience of receiving his Holy Spirit. John's gospel (20:22) has Jesus appear to the disciples on Easter Sunday evening and breathe on them, saying, "Receive the Holy Spirit."

As the Church instructs the neophytes (newly initiated) during the period of Mystagogy about the meaning of their sacramental initiation, she is in reality also instructing the rest of the faithful, who each year at Easter are asked to renew their baptismal promises. The Easter season is not just a commemoration of the Lord's resurrection. It is also a prolonged meditation on the *meaning* of the Lord's resurrection. And for the baptized, the key to that meaning lies in an exploration of the significance of their sacramental incorporation into the dying and rising of Jesus Christ. The three sacraments of Christian initiation—baptism, confirmation, and eucharist—are the focal points of the fifty days of Easter, because it is through those sacraments that every Christian comes to know the risen Christ in a deeply personal way. That is why so many parishes schedule their celebrations of First Eucharist and Confirmation during this time of year, and why infant baptisms are frequently given greater prominence by celebrating them at Mass during this time. The Easter season is a wonderful time to talk with children about the celebrations that marked their own baptism, confirmation, and first Eucharist, and to help them connect those celebrations to our faith in the Risen Christ.

Lent

The season of Lent in the new calendar lasts from Ash Wednesday up until the start of the Mass of the Lord's Supper on Holy Thursday. An older generation of believers delights in telling "war stories" about the rigors of Lent during their own childhood. No other liturgical season can match the deep impressions made on the young during Lent, with its ashes, its statues covered in purple, its fasting and its penances. But the focus of all that penitential discipline tended to be terribly individualistic and completely detached from the historical origins of the season. With the restoration of the catechumenate following the Second Vatican Council, the context for Lenten penance has been reestablished once again, and a much healthier communal perspective added.

The *Rite of Christian Initiation of Adults* (RCIA) has given us a new clarity and coherence about this season that is important for post-Vatican II Catholics to appreciate. In the RCIA the season of Lent is called the Period of Purification and Enlightenment. The two-fold emphasis this new terminology places both on penitential discipline (which "purifies") and other spiritual exercises (which bring "enlightenment") restores a much-needed balance to the season. Above all, the RCIA emphasizes that the reason for the community's participation in the season by embracing the discipline of Lent is so that they might experience solidarity with the elect who are preparing for initiation at the Easter Vigil. In the words of the *Rite* itself, "In the liturgy and the liturgical catechesis of Lent the reminder of baptism already received or the

71

preparation for its reception, as well as the theme of repentance, renew the entire community along with those being prepared to celebrate the paschal mystery, in which the elect will share through the sacraments of initiation. For both the elect and the local community, therefore, the Lenten season is a time for spiritual recollection in preparation for the celebration of the paschal mystery." (RCIA 138) The *Rite* makes it clear that an important way that members of the community engage in this process of preparation is by their actual participation in the catechumenal liturgies. "During Lent, the period of purification and enlightenment, the faithful should take care to participate in the rites of the scrutinies and presentations and give the elect the example of their own renewal in the spirit of penance, faith, and charity. At the Easter Vigil, they should attach great importance to renewing their own baptismal promises." (RCIA 9-4)

I can remember family discussions during my youth about what penances each of us children would adopt, usually giving up candy or movies and the like. But there was never any mention that the purpose of such penance was so that we might better renew the meaning of our own baptism at Easter, much less focus on the importance of the ritual renewal of baptismal vows which took place at all of the Masses of Easter. My hope is that future generations of children will be guided by their parents and teachers to understand the initiatory character of Lent, and why its discipline is focused on the Church's preparation for the paschal mystery above all in the celebration of the sacraments of Christian initiation. I would love to think of children, when they come to Mass on Ash Wednesday, being given photos of each of the members of the catechumenate who are to celebrate the Rite of Election with the bishop on the First Sunday of Lent. The children's parents and teachers would talk about those who will be initiated at the Easter Vigil in glowing terms, reminding them of how the community has witnessed and supported their growing faith in Jesus and their transformation into strong, faith-filled Christians. Children would be encouraged to pray for the elect, and their own voluntary penances would be offered up in support and love for those about to be born-again of water and Spirit. Families would plan on attending the Masses where the scrutinies would be celebrated on the third, fourth, and fifth Sundays of Lent, and the children would be told about the special rituals in which the elect would be presented with the Creed (during the third week of Lent) and the Our Father (during the fifth week of Lent) as core symbols of the faith they are about to profess. Catechesis of children at home and in school would center on helping them to prepare for the renewal of the baptismal promises that they would be asked to make at the Easter Vigil. Much as youngsters today are prepped in confirmation programs to make a personal decision about their faith, so the entire season of Lent would be focused on helping children prepare to stand up with the rest of the community on Easter and say personally the promises made on their behalf at their own baptism as infants.

We spoke in the previous chapter about how the Second Vatican Council saw as one of its most important challenges helping Catholics to recover an appreciation of baptism as the foundational sacrament of the Christian life. We can now appreciate even more deeply how central a role the sacred times of Lent, Triduum, and the Easter season are for the accomplishment of that aim. The Church wishes to "claim" those times as sacred, as a *kairos* of God's grace, and she does so first and foremost by structuring these liturgical seasons around the centrality of the paschal mystery. The *Constitution on the Sacred Liturgy* called for the renewal of each liturgical season, "so that they duly nourish the piety of the faithful who celebrate the mysteries of the Christian redemption and, above all, the paschal mystery." (107) During Lent, Triduum, and the Easter season, the Church helps us to see that the way we participate in Christ's paschal mystery is precisely through the three sacraments of Christian initiation, baptism, confirmation, and eucharist.

Advent

The weeks (perhaps, more accurately, the months!) prior to Christmas are usually a magical time for children as they anticipate the arrival of Santa Claus (or, if they are older, the "loot"). The barrage of advertising directed at children is incredibly intense, and those who market the consumer culture seem to outdo themselves every year with new and ingenious ways to associate the holidays in people's minds with spending more money than they had ever thought prudent. The escalating frenzy of our secularized version of Christmas celebrates the holiday before it arrives, with department store Santas, Christmas carols, pageants, decorations, and parties. Little wonder that by the time the liturgical season of Christmas begins, most of us are completely "spent" (in more ways than one) and eager to put it behind us.

Unless one chooses to insulate children entirely from our culture, there is probably little real chance of the liturgical season of Advent overwhelming the advertising blitzes of Madison Avenue with its own message. Nonetheless, the Church's approach to preparing for Christmas does offer something of real value amid so much materialistic display: A spiritual message that suggests the best way to prepare for Christmas lies in another direction from tinsel and conspicuous consumption. The natural openness of children gives us hope that they can hear this counter-claim if it is presented to them in reasonable fashion. Better to suggest that gift giving must include the poor than to condemn the toys and dolls that fill the TV screens. Better to talk in excited fashion about how Mary must have felt in the weeks before Jesus was born, than to rant about Santa as a secularized figure who perverts one of the holiest of Christian feast days. Children can hear a positive message, and the Church does indeed offer something of substance and value during the season of Advent.

There are always four Sundays of Advent. Depending on the day of the week on which Christmas falls, the fourth week of Advent may be shorter or longer. It is helpful to know that from the First Sunday of

Advent until December 16, the focus of the Church's prayers and readings is more on the second coming of Jesus than on his birth. This concern with the end times and his coming in glory is a fitting note to strike as the end of the calendar year approaches. After December 16, the focus shifts to a more direct preparation for the Lord's birth. The two comings—in glory at the end of time, and in the flesh in Bethlehem—are mingled together as part of a single mystery. We look forward to the former with longing and anticipation; we remember the latter with gratitude, and we prepare for its annual celebration with joyful expectancy.

Because the liturgical color for Advent is purple, and the Gloria is not sung during this time, it might seem that Advent is a penitential season. But the Roman calendar makes it quite clear that such is not the case. Advent, it says is "a season of joyful and spiritual expectation." (*Roman Calendar* 39) The absence of the Gloria and the wearing of purple are cues that the tone of the season is meant to be subdued, as befits a time of spiritual preparation. But it would be misleading to suggest that this is a time of penitential discipline. Rather, the focus is on intense spiritual preparation—as intense in its own right as are the materialistic preparations that are going forward in our secular society.

Children need to hear another message at this time of year than Santa Claus and shopping for gifts. Consider these possibilities:

- This is an excellent time to help prepare them in a special way to celebrate the Sacrament of Penance.

The positive message associated with preparing for Jesus' coming can be nicely wedded to preparations for the celebration of reconciliation.

- The liturgical readings about the final coming of Jesus allow us to explain that the reason for Jesus' first coming is so that when he comes in glory, he might bring salvation to the entire world.

- The notion of waiting for the Lord's coming can be linked to the many prophecies from the Jewish scriptures that are read at this time of year, helping children to appreciate the wonderful privilege that is ours to live in the time of fulfillment.

- This is also an excellent time of year to develop in children positive attitudes toward our sisters and brothers of Jewish faith, from whom the Messiah has come.

- It is also a wonderful opportunity to focus on a Marian piety that is linked to her role as the mother of the savior. Children know about pregnant mothers and the special time of waiting. They can identify with Mary's waiting, and in solidarity with her enter into a spirit of anticipation that is truly spiritual.

These are but a few of the ways that the themes of Advent can be made relevant to children. Though we might not be able to compete with Madison Avenue on its own turf, there certainly are a rich variety of ways that children can be connected to the proper spirit of Advent.

The Christmas Season

In the liturgical cycle, the most important feasts are prolonged for more than a single day. Like Easter, Christmas is celebrated with a vigil Mass and with its own octave (i.e., for eight days); and even after the octave is completed, the season further prolongs the celebration. The octave day of Christmas (January 1) is commemorated with the solemnity of Mary, mother of God, while the Sunday within the octave is celebrated as the feast of the Holy Family. The Christmas season also includes the solemnity of the Epiphany and the feast of the Baptism of the Lord.

This tremendous richness reflects a long historical evolution in which many different traditions of the Church have come together around one of our most central doctrines, the Incarnation. Christian belief that Jesus is the son of God, truly human and truly divine, is a truth so profound that there is little wonder we should have a myriad of feasts celebrating various facets of the mystery.

Children, of course, are drawn to and marvel at the infant born in a stable, and the Christmas story is a narrative that never ceases to engage the imaginations of young and old alike. But it is important not to sell children short in their ability to explore and contemplate the theological depth of this mystery. The Incarnation is a truth whose ramifications are literally inexhaustible, and to have children think of nothing more than the cute baby in a manger is to nourish them on meager fare. The multiple celebrations that make up the Christmas season allow us to explore with children the holiness of family life, Mary's role in God's plan of salvation, as well as the striking truth of the universality of God's salvific will. In the Baptism of the Lord we are even invited to explore the notion of Jesus' anointing by the Holy Spirit for his saving mission. Taking time with children to explore each of the major feasts of the Christmas season will yield enormous dividends by enriching their grasp of the breadth of what the Incarnation is truly about.

Ordinary Time

Apart from the liturgical seasons discussed above, there are thirty-three or thirty-four weeks of the year that are called Ordinary Time. These begin in January at the end of the Christmas season and continue until Ash Wednesday. Ordinary Time then resumes when the Easter season ends in May or June, and it runs until the First Sunday of Advent. The liturgical color associated with Ordinary Time is green.

Throughout Ordinary Time, both on Sundays and weekdays, the Lectionary contains continuous cycles of various readings from the Gospels and New Testament. The statement in the *Constitution on the Sacred Liturgy* that "in the course of the year" the liturgical cycle "unfolds the whole mystery of Christ" (102) refers not only to the special seasons discussed above which have a particular doctrinal focus. The *Constitution* also intends to refer to Ordinary Time, which reveals to the faithful the vast scope of the Christian mystery by the many different themes that are present, both in the course of its regular celebrations and in the particular feasts that occur during this time.

Robert D. Duggan

The Church sees regular participation in the liturgy throughout the year as a powerful form of both evangelization and catechesis. The proclamation of God's word in the Lectionary is a particularly important source of both of these activities of the Church. In the Apostolic Constitution (April 3, 1969) promulgating the revised Roman Missal, Pope Paul VI commented on the hope of the Second Vatican Council that the Scriptures proclaimed in the Lectionary would be for future generations "a perpetual source of the spiritual life, the chief instrument for handing down Christian doctrine, and the center of all theological study." It is for this reason that many communities make the Scriptures proclaimed at the Sunday celebrations throughout the year the basis for the instruction that is offered both to those in the catechumenate and to young people in religious education programs.

There is nothing ordinary about Ordinary Time. To live the rhythms of the Church's liturgy throughout the year is to enter a world of grace, where each week there are revelations of God's miraculous love for his people. In the assembly gathered—week in and week out—to offer worship and praise, young people are formed in the meaning of Christian community. They discover the importance of relationships that develop gradually over time; they learn about the Church's commitment to work for justice and peace, and they see in practice the meaning of charity toward the poor and needy. In the midst of the liturgical assembly, young people absorb our specifically Catholic identity, with its distinctive attitudes and values. A gospel ethic of respect for life—from the first moment of conception to natural death—is assimilated "with the air they breathe," whether that air is perfumed with incense and beeswax candles, the sweat of poor folks jammed into an aging church without air conditioning, or the smell of soap on fresh-scrubbed suburbanites. Children for whom the Church's liturgy is experienced not as something they must "do," but rather as "who we are," will carry the impact of those hundreds and hundreds of celebrations that take place during the "ordinary" times of their youth with them for the rest of their lives.

Parents and teachers should help children understand how important it is to participate fully, consciously and actively in the Church's liturgical life all year-round, not just on the "high holy days" of Christmas and Easter. To live the spirit of the liturgy at a deep level, one must feel the importance of Ordinary Time just as strongly as Lent or Easter or Christmas. Family customs of prayer that reflect the changing liturgical rhythms are important in this regard. During Ordinary Time there needs to be a core of household prayer patterns that constitutes the "domestic liturgy" of the "domestic church," and that are consistent with what is unfolding in the Church's public worship. One of the concerns of the bishops at the Second Vatican Council was that the devotional life of Catholics would be brought more closely into harmony with the Church's official liturgy. Family customs of prayer should take their cue from the "shape" of the Church's official life of prayer in the liturgy. One of the most popular ways this happens is through what is called the "Sanctoral cycle" that runs concurrently with the seasonal cycle discussed above.

The Sanctoral Cycle

The liturgical year is made up of the Proper of the Seasons and the Proper of the Saints, which is also called the Sanctoral cycle. The reform of the Roman calendar after the Second Vatican Council continued the age-old custom of honoring the saints with a system of annual celebrations of various ranks and degrees of importance. [The new terminology in the reformed calendar has three basic designations: Solemnities, Feasts, and Memorials (which are either obligatory or optional).] By the time of the Council, the Sanctoral cycle had grown unwieldy over the centuries, and its system of classifying the relative importance of various celebrations lacked coherence. Thus, the reformed calendar attempts to bring order and consistency to the way that the Church honors the saints. Solemnities of the Lord (Corpus Christi, Sacred Heart, Christ the King, and so forth), of course, take precedence over all other feasts. Mary retains a place of honor among all of the saints, while the dates and degrees of importance of the celebrations honoring other saints were adjusted in many instances. The Roman calendar continues to change because the process of canonization regularly adds saints whose memory is to be celebrated in the universal Church.

The Roman calendar contains the official listing of the festival days for those saints who are to be honored liturgically in the universal Church. The Roman Martyrology, on the other hands, is the listing of all of the saints' names handed down by centuries of Christian tradition. Many of the names and exploits of saints in the Martyrology are judged to be of questionable historicity, and so they do not have a designated celebration in the universal calendar. But the Roman calendar also acknowledges that dioceses and regions may wish to develop their own, adapted calendars to reflect the appeal of certain local saints held in particularly high esteem.

There are certain days that are designated as "holy days of obligation" because of their importance as festivals of the Church. On those days Catholics are obliged to participate in the Eucharist as a way of acknowledging the significance of the celebration. Conferences of bishops are given the option of lifting the precept of obligatory Eucharist on certain of those days, or of transferring the observance to the nearest Sunday. Thus, the list of "holy days" observed in particular regions changes from time to time and from locality to locality. Nonetheless, the notion of what a holy day is all about is something that is important for children to learn. Youngsters know that it is important to celebrate family members' birthdays or their parents' wedding anniversary. They "have to" participate in the celebration, not under duress or constraint, but because of the bonds of love that they know need to be expressed in explicit fashion. In much the same way, children can be led to understand that holy days of obligation "have to" be celebrated because they represent God's love for us in particularly important ways, a love that we "must" reciprocate and celebrate.

The Sanctoral cycle represents the Church's acknowledgement of the importance of popular devotion to sustain and nourish faith. Children love heroes, and they need to be able to identify with men and women—and even children—who share situations like their own, and who inspire by their examples of courage and love.

We mentioned above that the Sanctoral cycle is an important way that the domestic church of the home can celebrate the rhythms of the Church's liturgy on a scale that is manageable and intelligible to children. Above all, children should be helped to develop a warm and deep affection for our blessed Mother. Mary's role in the story of our salvation is unique, and children should be helped to appreciate that uniqueness. They need also to cultivate a personal relationship with Mary in prayer, learning of her intercessory powers and being sustained by her example of openness and obedience to God's will. The place of the rosary in fostering this devotion is unrivaled in our Catholic tradition.

The doctrine of the Communion of Saints is a heady theological notion for children. But they can experience this truth long before they learn its technical name, simply by being introduced to the stories of the saints and learning how to pray to them for their help in times of need. Children should learn about their patron saints. When a new child is born into a family, imagine how wonderful it would be to discuss the new baby's name in light of the virtues that its patron saint displayed. As the feast days of various saints approach, children can be told the stories of the saints' lives. They can learn about the saints by doing projects that help them appreciate better the ways that God's grace works in ordinary people like us.

The Liturgy of the Hours

One of the strongest images I have of priests from my childhood is seeing them walking back and forth in their long black cassocks, reading from a black prayer book with many ribbons. That prayer book, the Breviary, was a mysterious Latin text that every Catholic knew belonged only to the ordained. For those who knew its technical name, the Divine Office, the priest's prayer book seemed even more beyond the reach of the average Catholic. Little wonder, then, that many were shocked at these words from the *Constitution on the Sacred Liturgy*: "The laity, too, are encouraged to recite the divine office, either with the priests, or among themselves, or even individually." (100)

In order to encourage this dramatic shift in perception, the Divine Office was restructured, simplified, and, of course, published in vernacular editions. A new name, the Liturgy of the Hours, was also given to this prayer to emphasize that it is a prayer designed to accompany certain designated times of day. The remarks we made at the start of this chapter about the nature of sacred time are relevant here. The Liturgy of the Hours is the Church's "everyday" attempt to reclaim each hour of the day as *kairos*, as a time of grace in which the Lord may be encountered. As the *Constitution* states, "The purpose of the office is to sanctify the day." (88) The ideal, of course, is that the Hours be prayed in a communal setting (99), since it is "the public prayer of the Church." (90) The *Constitution* calls it "the voice of the Church, that is, of the whole mystical body publicly praising God." (99) In its renewed form, the two principal parts of the Liturgy of the Hours, the "hinges" so to speak, are Morning Prayer and Evening Prayer.

We still have a long way to go before a substantial number of Catholics shares the Council's vision of the Liturgy of the Hours as the prayer of the whole Church, rather than a monastic or priestly prayer. But we should remember how far we have already come since the Council's startling statement that the laity should be encouraged to pray the office. It may not be so unrealistic after all to think that today's children will live in a Church where *all* of the People of God have learned to make some form of the Liturgy of the Hours part of their "daily prayer." More and more parishes are using forms of prayer based on the Liturgy of the Hours to begin and end their meetings or other gatherings. Popular adaptations are readily available for use by individuals or families. In some communities, during special seasons like Advent and Lent, sung versions of the Liturgy of the Hours are being celebrated publicly on a routine basis.

The outlook is hopeful, then, that future generations will "own" this prayer and make it as much a part of their devotional life as the rosary or a visit to the blessed Sacrament. Parents and teachers can help children in this direction by seeing to it that they become familiar with the simple format of the Liturgy of the Hours. The prominence of the psalms in the prayer means that we need to help children become familiar with how to pray the psalms as their own. Likewise, we need to foster an attitude of praise in the prayer of the young, since the dominant mood of the Liturgy of the Hours is one of praise. Nothing, of course, will be as effective in helping children to embrace this prayer as their own as the actual experience of praying the Hours with adults who are significant figures for them. When parents, teachers, youth leaders, and other prominent members of the community are observed praying the Hours—and when they make sure that the young are included—then our children will learn at the deepest possible level that this prayer, indeed, belongs to them.

3

The Eucharist, Source and Summit of the Christian Life

Source and Summit

These two terms, source and summit, have proven to be among the most often quoted words of any of the documents of the Second Vatican Council. In both the *Constitution on the Sacred Liturgy* (10) and the *Dogmatic Constitution on the Church* (11), the bishops of the Council taught that the Eucharist is the fountain from which flows all of the Church's life and power, as well as the aim towards which all of her activity is directed. Truly, the Eucharist stands at the heart of our Catholic tradition of faith. There can be no catechetical task that is more urgent than preparing children to participate fully, consciously, and actively in that which is the source and summit of their Christian existence. That having been said, however, it is quite another thing to identify just what is needed in order to prepare them adequately to participate in the eucharistic assembly.

What must we do to prepare them adequately?

The parish in which I presently minister has used a multipurpose building as its primary place of worship since 1975. Because of the many different activities that take place in that space, the blessed Sacrament is not reserved there, and the movable chairs that are in use do not allow for kneeling during our eucharistic celebrations. Thus, there are many children in the parish who have grown up without a regular experience of genuflecting to the blessed Sacrament and who have no experience of the community kneeling together as part of their eucharistic worship.

Shortly after I first arrived as pastor, the bishop was scheduled to come for the annual confirmation of our youth. It was a new bishop who had never been to the parish before, and his master of ceremonies advised me when he arrived that the bishop preferred to have the children kneel before his chair so that he could confirm from a seated position. I told one of the catechists to inform the youngsters of that fact and thought nothing further about it. The very first child to come forward stopped in front of the bishop, went down on all fours, and raised up his forehead like a dog, waiting to be patted on the head. I was too stunned to burst out laughing, thank God, but I still did not understand what was about to unfold. The very next child, who had obviously observed the awkwardness of her predecessor, squatted before his excellency as if to relieve herself! My amusement turned to horror, as I suddenly realized, *These children don't know how to kneel down!* I'm certain the remaining anointings with chrism did not last for hours, though it seemed like it to me, as I watched fully half of the confirmands take one strange posture after another, trying to figure out how to kneel down before the bishop's chair. *What must we do to prepare them adequately?* I learned a great deal on that day—a day I will surely never forget—about the need for a careful and comprehensive preparation of children so that they can participate meaningfully in our liturgical rituals.

I can look back with humor now on the disaster that happened at that confirmation day nearly fifteen years ago. But the tragic element that it represents continues to haunt me. What else did we "miss" in those children's religious training, a training which ostensibly was preparing them to take their place among the fully initiated at the Eucharistic assembly? Too often, I continue to encounter children well along in elementary school who seem totally unaware of the most fundamental elements of our liturgical tradition. I see children who do not know that they are supposed to make the sign of cross when a priest raises his hands and offers a blessing, "In the name of the Father, and . . ." Or, there are those who know they're supposed to do "something" with their hands, but who miss (or mix up the proper order of) most of the four bases they're supposed to touch as they bless themselves. I've given a church tour to a class of fourth graders and discovered that only one child knew what the tabernacle was; only three could tell me about the connection between holy water and baptism. *What must we do to prepare them adequately?*

The issue, in my judgement, is not a trivial one, because the liturgy continues to be the Church's primary vehicle for passing on the faith. Without in any way wishing to minimize the importance of our formal cate-chetical efforts, it simply has always been the case (and, I believe, always will be) that participation in the liturgy shapes our Catholic mind and heart far more profoundly than any other single element of our multi-faceted exposure to Catholicism. Preparing children *adequately*, so that they can enter deeply into the eucharistic liturgy, is a "mission-critical" task of religious educators and parents alike. Now, let us explore a bit more carefully what is implied in that key word, "adequately."

Ritual Competency

Anyone familiar with how our public education system works in the United States knows that its overall aim is to prepare citizens for participation in our democratic society. To achieve this aim, a carefully developed learning curriculum has been put together. All of the resources of the teaching profession have been marshaled to help children master a progressively more sophisti-cated series of competencies, so that when they "graduate" they will have the knowledge and skills necessary to participate fully and effectively within our society. The elaborate system of tests that are part of the educational experience is designed to measure to what degree children have, in fact, achieved those competencies.

I first heard the expression "ritual competency" in a talk by the Dominican theologian Paul Philibert, and it remains an intriguing notion that continues to challenge my thinking about how we can adequately prepare children to participate in the eucharistic liturgy. The idea of ritual competency, as I have come to think of it, is analogous to what our secular education system is doing to prepare children for participation in our democratic society. There, the aim is participation in our democracy. In the case of ritual competency, the aim is participation in the Church's liturgy. Just what is it, I ask myself, that children must be able to do in order to participate in the eucharistic liturgy as they ought? The answer to that question represents a series of ritual competencies that our children need to master.

Discussing the renewal of the liturgy, the *Constitution on the Sacred Liturgy* said that the *aim to be considered before all else* is "full and active participation by all the people." The *Constitution* even goes on to explain that the reason for making the people's participation such an overriding priority is because the liturgy "is the primary and indispensable source from which the faithful are to derive the true Christian spirit." (14)

The Council Fathers' use of the phrase "full, conscious, and active participation of all the faithful" as the aim of the entire liturgical renewal was not a matter of chance; nor did they choose that expression heedless of its implications. Some version of the phrase, in fact, appears numerous times throughout the *Constitution*. By the time of the Council, the phrase had already appeared in church documents for more than half a century. Pope Pius X had first used it at the turn of the century, and subsequently both popes and theologians had often repeated the expression, further elaborating on its implications. Generations of scholars and pastoral workers had used "full, conscious, and active participation" as a rallying cry for the liturgical renewal. In short, it was an expression whose content and implications were well known to the Council Fathers.

But despite the clarity that existed in the minds of the bishops at the Vatican Council, for us there still remains an enormous amount of work to be done to identify the specific ritual competencies that a child must master in order to attain that goal. In recent years the United States' bishops have put a great deal of time and effort into developing a protocol, based on the *Catechism of the Catholic Church*, for publishers of religious education texts, in which they spell out in detailed fashion the doctrines that a child should know and understand at each grade level through elementary school. Their goal, apparently, was to ensure that children achieve a certain level of competency, a religious literacy, in the area of Catholic doctrine, by the time they graduate from elementary school. However, to my knowledge there does not exist any comparable source (or even any coherent vision, however incomplete its articulation may be) that spells out the competencies required to equip a child to participate meaningfully in the Sunday Eucharist as a fully initiated Catholic.

The suggestions offered below as to what those competencies might be do not pretend to be exhaustive, nor have they been elaborated with the kind of extensive process of consultation reflected in the *Catechism* and the bishops' protocol. But they do represent a start, and hopefully they will stimulate further thought about how we can better prepare children to participate in the eucharist "fully, consciously, and actively." Such participation is their baptismal birthright, their priestly office of worship, which they exercise each and every time they offer the sacrifice of the Mass. It is incumbent upon us to identify with some precision the ritual competencies they need to master in order to achieve that kind of participation. Let's look more closely now at just what some of those competencies are.

Ritual Competency #1: They need to know the stories.

Children need to know the biblical stories that comprise our collective memory as the people of God. They need to know the characters, their personalities, and the twists and turns of plots that reveal not only the tragedy of human sinfulness, but the amazing grace of our God, the God of covenant love. They need to know these stories not only to be able to make sense out of the little snippets that we read from the Lectionary. They need to know them also because virtually all of the prayers we say at Mass draw on the imagery and stories of faith that make up some of our most exciting biblical narratives. Imagine how little sense the following section from Eucharistic Prayer I would make to a child who did not know the biblical stories to which it alludes: *Look with favor on these offerings and accept them as once you accepted the gifts of your servant Abel, the sacrifice of Abraham our father in faith, and the bread and wine offered by your priest Melchisedech.* Unless a child has "gotten the point" of the story of Cain and Abel, it will make no sense to ask God to accept *this* offering as he did Abel's. Unless a child has listened with rapt attention to the tale of Abraham trudging up the mountain to slay his only son, it makes no sense to ask God that *this* offering will be accepted in the same spirit of absolute faith. Unless one has heard of the mysterious figure of Melchisedech, whose simple offering of gifts became so much more, then there will be no glimmer of recognition as this prayer is prayed.

Children need to know the bible stories that tell us who we are as a people and that reveal to us the God whom we have come to know and love in Jesus his son. If children do not know the stories as *their stories*, then when they are at liturgy they will stand apart and listen as if to something that has little or nothing to do with their own lives.

Robert D. Duggan

Ritual Competency #2: They need to know the symbols.

Liturgy uses the language of symbol and ritual, a kind of "code language" that only the initiated can fully understand. A Buddhist child in China who has never been exposed to Christianity will see bread and wine on an altar table and think that someone is preparing a meal, nothing more. It is only when children have been initiated into our symbol system that they can participate fully in the ritual action of the liturgy and in the meanings represented by our symbolic language. Children need to be familiarized with the associations that give meaning to the primary symbols of our liturgical tradition: bread and wine, oil and water, sacred touch, fire/light, the gathered assembly, and so forth.

It is the wedding of story with symbol that "layers" meanings and makes liturgical symbols so inexhaustibly rich. When a Catholic child sees someone immersed in baptismal water at the Easter Vigil, one would hope that the rite evokes in the child's mind associations with the story of Noah and the waters of the flood, the waters of the Red Sea which parted to allow God's people to pass through to freedom, the Jordan River which they crossed over to the Promised Land, and in which Jesus himself was baptized. When that child feels the baptismal water being sprinkled on her own face after the renewal of baptismal promises, we can only pray that her associations are something more than her little brother squirting her with a water pistol!

Children need to know the symbols, what they represent, the stories that give them meaning, and the ways that our rituals use those symbols to celebrate God's grace in our midst. Imagine a child who has witnessed his mother—recently diagnosed with cancer—being anointed generously with oil in the sacrament of the sick, surrounded by a church full of people on Sunday morning who pray for her, many of whom come forward to lay hands on her along with the priest. For that child, oil will forevermore hold new associations of prayer for healing and comforting touch. And, to be sure, those associations will allow that child in the future to participate much more fully when he is present at a Mass where the Sacrament of Anointing is celebrated.

Ritual Competency #3: They need to know their "cues."

One of the most painful experiences I have from time to time as a priest is to celebrate the funeral rites with a family, ostensibly Catholic, but in fact so unchurched that they do not know even the most basic liturgical "cues." When I say "The Lord be with you," and receive back only confused stares, I know for certain that the potential comfort and consolation that the ritual could offer is largely going to be "missed" by the family.

If children are truly to "belong" and be at home in our liturgical assemblies, they need to be familiar with the "cues" that tell them what is happening and what their role in the ritual action should be. Something inside of me cringes when a child (or even an adult!) comes forward to receive Holy Communion, and instead of saying "Amen" and stretching out a hand or tongue, just smiles at me and says "thanks," without any effort to receive reverently what I offer as "the Body of Christ." Full, conscious, and active participation requires that liturgical cues have become part of our very being, not something we have to think about or fumble over. When the responsorial psalm is sung in antiphonal fashion with the cantor, and a large part of the assembly is not even attempting to participate in the response, the community's prayer is weakened, and God's people fail to offer the fitting praise for which they have gathered. Children need to know that the cantor's invocation of the psalm refrain is their cue to respond, and that failure to respond compromises the prayer of the body of Christ!

Ritual Competency #4: They need to know the "body language" of worship.

In my hospital ministry, I have often anointed an elderly person who was deep in a coma, unresponsive, and at the point of death. On more than one occasion, as I have given the blessing, "In the name of the Father, and of the Son . . ." the comatose individual has raised a hand and blessed himself or herself in unison with my words. On such occasions, I know for certain that our Catholic liturgical tradition has so permeated that person's life as to have entered and become part of their very being, even on a physical level. They *know* the "body language" of worship; and their body, in turn, *knows* what it means to pray.

This is as it ought to be. In many respects, I consider this an image of the "ideal" toward which we ought to strive as we teach children the body language of worship. Our Christian faith is incarnational, and the sacramentality of our Catholic tradition is its most distinctive feature. We "embody" our experience of the divine, first and foremost in Jesus the Christ, and because of him in the body of Christ, the Church. Our incarnational faith is evident in our belief in the seven sacraments of the New Covenant, and in the sacramentals that are so much a part of the fabric of our Catholic devotional life.

I remember as a young child going to a movie, walking down the rows of seats in the theater, and upon reaching the row where I was going to sit, genuflecting before entering. I was, of course, horrified with embarrassment once I realized what I had done. My body's "automatic response" had betrayed me, given me away in that secular arena as a Catholic. Now I can laugh about it, but in a way I wish every Catholic child would so absorb the "body language" of our worship that such impulses are just below the surface of conscious awareness at all times. Genuflection, making the sign of the cross, bowing one's head, kneeling, raising hands and arms in prayer—all of these and more are the language of our body at prayer, and children need to so assimilate these practices that they can "speak the language" fluently and with the eloquence of an accomplished conversationalist.

Ritual Competency #5: They need to understand the structure and flow of the Eucharist.

The repetitive nature of the eucharistic liturgy makes it very easy for children to become familiar with the structure of the ritual. There is an integrity to the parts and how they fit together that gives the celebration a kind of organic unity. We begin with gathering rites, and these involve a degree of variety from week to week. The heart of the celebration is when the assembly is nourished at the table of the word and the table of the Lord's body and blood. And then our closing rites always end with a sending forth, a mandate to go in peace to make a difference in the world to which we return. Children need to learn about this structure, not as an object of abstract study, but as a certain rhythm that "makes sense" to them because they have absorbed its own internal logic.

Knowing the "flow" of a ritual refers to the intuitive feel we develop for how the parts unfold one after the other. It's the knowledge that a good ballroom dancer has for the music. The dancer may not be able to read a musical score or tell you anything at all about musical theory, but he or she knows the flow, the rhythms that must be followed in order to be a graceful part of the experience. A child needs to be so sensitively attuned to the "flow" of the eucharistic liturgy that to arrive late or to leave before the end of the closing song becomes unthinkable, an aberration to be avoided at all costs. I once attended a "home Mass" in a parishioner's basement, presided over by their five-year-old son who had created a makeshift church with an eye to detail that stunned me. He knew everything that was supposed to happen, and he gave ferocious directions to his three-year-old brother whenever the little one got out of line and interrupted the flow of the celebration. I learned an important lesson there in that contemporary catacomb about how much children are capable of learning about the eucharistic ritual when they have a natural interest that is nourished by supportive parents.

Ritual Competency #6: They need to know the "script."

Ritual competency requires that children master their part of the "script" of the celebration. By this I refer to both the spoken and sung texts that allow one to participate fully and actively. This involves knowing "by heart"—in the true sense of that expression—such prayers as the Gloria, the Creed, the Our Father, as well as the shorter responses and acclamations. The ability of children to learn music is phenomenal, and they love to participate in community song. We do them a disservice by exposing them only to "children's music" that we think will appeal more because it is simpler. We should help them learn the words and their meanings right from the beginning, so that they will not discover at age ten or eleven that the Our Father is not saying, "Our Father who march in heaven . . . deliver us from eagle . . ." Adults find such mistakes delightfully cute, but we do children a disservice when we fail to help them learn the ritual script correctly from the beginning.

Robert D. Duggan

Ritual Competency #7: They need to know that participation in the eucharistic ritual has ethical implications.

Sacred ritual always has an implicit message about how we should live our lives. Those who know about the role that eating with the outcast played in the ministry of Jesus must be attuned to the deeper significance of his command at the Last Supper, when he washed the disciples' feet and said, "Do this in memory of me." Children need to understand that the link between liturgy and life is seamless. One does not exchange a sign of peace with the person next to you at eucharist and then ridicule him on the playground the next day because his skin is a different color than yours. One does not pray for the poor at the general intercessions and then engage in business practices that exploit the poor. One does not lightly pray with the rest of the community, "forgive us our trespasses as we forgive those . . ." and then vote for a candidate simply because she promises to "get tough" on criminals and promote the death penalty.

Children need to be told that the eucharist commits us to a particular way of being in the world, to a set of values and an attitude towards all of life's important issues. It is because we are disciples of Jesus Christ that we participate in the eucharist, and that sets us apart. We need to help children ask the "so what" question at deeper and deeper levels. So, what difference, *does* it make that I share eucharist? And what *is* the significance of the words I say and the actions I perform at eucharist? Learning to ask questions about the implications of our ritual behavior needs to be a deeply ingrained habit in children, lest they grow up thinking that religion and the sacraments are all terribly irrelevant to real life. Of course, once we encourage such questioning, it is not long before we adults become uncomfortable with the way we are challenged by children's questions that reveal the disparity between what we proclaim in church and the reality of our lives. But we must not stifle children's challenging questions simply to make ourselves more comfortable.

Ritual Competency #8: They need to be able to recognize the "holy presence."

The core of the experience of worship is the knowledge that one is in the presence of the holy. Our Catholic tradition affirms that, by virtue of baptism, each of us has become a temple of the Holy Spirit. At the deepest level of who we are, there dwells the mystery of a divine presence, a union of our spirit with the all-holy God. We bring that awareness to worship; and, as deep calls unto deep, so the Spirit within calls out to the holy presence that surrounds us when the Church is at prayer. The *Constitution on the Sacred Liturgy* specified the manifold ways that Christ is present in the eucharistic celebration: He is present in the person of the priest who presides; in his word "since it is he himself who speaks when the holy Scriptures are read in the Church;" in the assembly gathered; and, "especially in the eucharistic species." (7) Reading Matthew 25, we might also add that in the outcast, the stranger, and all who are afflicted, we also recognize a special presence of the suffering Christ.

We must help children to recognize all of these ways that we are in the presence of the holy when we gather for liturgy. If we have a precious memento of an ancestor—say, a delicate porcelain teacup of our great, great grandmother—we are careful to teach children to treat it with care and respect. Just so, we help children to develop a sense of sacred presence, and we teach them what constitutes a proper attitude and proper behavior in one who recognizes that holy presence.

Ritual Competency #9: They need to be comfortable with many different kinds of prayer.

Our Catholic tradition of prayer is rich and varied. The *Catechism of the Catholic Church* spells out the many forms that our prayer takes: blessing, adoration, petition, intercession, thanksgiving, and praise. (2623-49) One can also speak of the different expressions of prayer: vocal prayer, meditation, and contemplative prayer. (2700-24) We need to recognize that this diversity of form and expression is characteristic of the eucharist as well. Above all, the eucharist (Greek = thanksgiving) is a prayer of thanks and praise. But there are moments during the eucharist in which we ask forgiveness, as well as times that call for contemplative silence. There are times that call for the exuberance of communal praise, as well as times where the appropriate prayer is a quiet, individual petition for God's grace.

Children need to be broadly schooled in the ways of prayer, so that they are open to and capable of praying in all of these ways. Someone needs to explain to them at what points in the eucharistic ritual certain kinds of prayer are called for. When the community rises to its feet to greet Christ in the gospel by singing "Alleluia," it is not an appropriate time for a private confession of sin. Or, when the assembly joins in singing a song to accompany the communion procession, it is not time for silent meditation. We enhance the ritual competency of children by making them comfortable with the broadest possible repertoire of Christian prayer and by teaching them to recognize when each form is appropriate in the eucharistic ritual.

This is not an easy task. In our contemporary culture, the art of contemplative silence, for example, does not come easily to children who are bombarded with constant noise and the rush of digital images. Helping children learn how to listen to the proclaimed word with a contemplative openness, and how to allow that word to be planted deeply in the heart where it rests in the stillness, is to teach a skill that little else in our culture offers them.

Ritual Competency #10: They must know the need for a savior.

The entire premise on which the eucharist is based requires an awareness of our need for a savior. We feel little reason to be thankful to one who gives us what we already have. On the other hand, to be lost, powerless, hopeless, and then to be offered an unexpected and undeserved way out, is to have found a truly amazing grace. Such an experience leads one to a deep spirit of gratitude and thankfulness. Church leaders have lamented for many years now the loss of a sense of sin among the young. They perceive, and rightly so, that a person who has no sense of sin or guilt feels no need for forgiveness, no openness to the gift of God's saving grace. The penitential rite at the beginning of Mass simply makes no sense to one who does not acknowledge responsibility for being a sinner.

We must help children to develop a proper sense of sin and guilt. That does not mean we leave them with a burden of shame. On the contrary, only true guilt can accept forgiveness; shame refuses the gift of God's pardon. In developing an awareness of our need for a savior, we must also introduce children to the notion of social sin. The horrific evils of genocide, the corrupt exercise of power on a massive scale, greed that is sometimes global in reach; these are conditions of social sin that would cause despair were it not for our conviction that Jesus Christ has triumphed over all of the powers of sin and evil in the world. Children are keenly sensitive to many of these realities, and that sensitivity can provide an opening to the Christian understanding of the cosmic triumph of Christ's paschal mystery.

Children must bring to the eucharist an awareness of their own need—and the need of the entire world—for Jesus Christ as Lord and Savior. Aware of that need, they are then in a position to say with a depth of meaning and conviction, "Lord, I am not worthy . . . but only say the word and I shall be healed." Once they have grasped the helplessness of the human condition to rise above its own slavery to sin, *then* they are in a position to understand why we so desperately need Jesus and the forgiveness and healing that he alone can bring. We need to connect children to that grace, both in terms of their own struggle with sin, and in light of the overwhelming realities of social sin in the world. In both cases, they must be helped to recognize, it is Jesus alone who can rescue us from our helplessness and slavery to sin.

Ritual Competency #11: They need to be developing a healthy psychosocial maturity.

Scholastic theologians of the Middle Ages used to say, "Grace builds on nature." Although they did not possess the sophisticated knowledge of human growth and development that the modern social sciences provide, they did recognize a very basic truth. Unless children grow in healthy ways, their capacity for a healthy spiritual life is compromised. Erik Erikson talked about the importance of developing early on in life a fundamental trust. Without that, one's ability to enter into relationship is damaged. Without trust, one cannot risk self-disclosure, and the defenses are too high to allow one to go out of oneself and really *encounter* the other.

All of this is quite relevant to the process of spiritual maturation that should parallel a child's human growth and development. Religion is about relationships, first with God and secondly with one's neighbors, as the great commandment of Jesus clearly indicates. (Matthew 22:37-39) One of the fundamental competencies required for liturgical participation is the ability to enter into healthy relationships, first with God and secondly with the community that gathers to worship. We must attend to the issue of psychosocial development in children, lest there arise stumbling blocks to their ability to worship in a healthy manner. We know how true this is from dramatic instances, such as young girls sexually abused by their fathers. The emotional damage of such abuse most often makes it nearly impossible for them to relate to God as a benevolent Father.

Even apart from such dramatic situations, we should recognize how healthy growth and development of children on a psychosocial level forms the basis for the development of a sound spiritual life. And, a robust spiritual life is the basis in turn for liturgical participation that is healthy. An example of this is a child's capacity for selflessness, which is possible only in the context of an integrated personality structure where one's basic needs have been met. That capacity for selflessness is what makes a child capable of the virtue of self-sacrifice, which of course is at the heart of the notion of offering. When we suggest that we "offer" the Mass in union with Christ's offering, we tap into a key element in the spiritual life. Self-sacrificial offering, in obedience to the Father's will, was the essence of Christ's sacrifice on the cross. Our capacity to embrace a similar stance is crucial for our ability to offer ourselves in union with Christ's self-offering. The emotional capacity for selflessness makes possible the Christian virtue of self-sacrifice, and the virtue of self-sacrifice in turn is a ritual competency that makes possible meaningful participation in the Eucharist as a sacrificial offering of self in union with Christ.

Ritual Competency #12: They need to understand that the liturgy is public, not private prayer.

The liturgy is the public worship of the Church, and as such its nature is communal and social. There are certainly individual and private dimensions to one's participation in the liturgy, but the *Constitution on the Sacred Liturgy* went to great pains to emphasize that "Liturgical services are not private functions but are celebrations of the Church." (26) The bishops went on to insist, "It must be emphasized that rites which are meant to be celebrated in common, with the faithful present and actively participating, should as far as possible be celebrated in that way. . . . This applies with special force to the celebration of Mass." (27)

Children are certainly influenced by the religious privatism and individualism that is so deeply embedded in our American culture. The idea that one must let go of one's own preferences and tastes for the sake of the common good is not something that we come to easily. Add to that a consumer culture, where one expects to be entertained, and it becomes clear why the formation of proper attitudes in children for worship is a formidable task indeed. The "success" of the Church's public prayer depends on the active participation of everyone in the assembly. To withdraw for reasons of personal piety, or to participate only to a limited degree because a particular musical or homiletic style does not suit our tastes, is to miss the point of our responsibility for the common good. We are present in the liturgical assembly to give God worship, to offer our best like Abel, not our grudging second best like Cain. When we stand apart from the liturgical action to observe, critique or judge it, we disengage from the active participation that is required of us. Children need to learn that we come to liturgy to "give," not to "get," though of course the result is always that we "get" far, far more than we "give." Children must also be convinced of the importance of their presence, their attention, the engagement of their whole heart and mind, in the public act of worship. *That* they are present, and *how* they are present matters, and we need to instill in them a keen awareness of that fact.

Ritual Competency #13: They need to know the basic theology of Eucharist.

The emphasis in this chapter has not been on the Church's tradition of doctrinal reflection on the mystery of the eucharist. This choice should in no way be construed as an indication that it is unimportant for children to have a thorough understanding of our Catholic theology of the eucharist. Quite to the contrary, it is very important that children have an age-appropriate grasp of the way that we Catholics have reflected on and come to understand the mystery of the Holy Eucharist. The *Catechism of the Catholic Church* (1322-1419) has an excellent summary for adults of Catholic doctrine on the eucharist. Both catechists and parents will find there a treatment that is remarkably straightforward. The contents will, of course, have to be conveyed to children gradually and in ways that they are capable of assimilating. But the outline of the essential truths that children need to understand is quite clearly laid out.

Children should know that we understand the eucharist as both a sacrifice and a sacrament, as a memorial of the Lord's passion, and as a sacred banquet. They should know about the preparation for this sacrament in the Jewish Scriptures, and its institution in the New Covenant. The *Catechism* offers a particularly lucid explanation of the liturgy of the eucharist, the parts of the Mass and the movement of the celebration. Children need to know about the hierarchical nature of our worship, the essential role played by an ordained priest who acts in the person of Christ, as well as the common priesthood of the baptized that empowers them to offer the eucharist in union with the ordained minister. They should also understand the various ministries that they see exercised in a eucharistic celebration, and in particular, they should appreciate the significance of their own ministry as a member of the assembly.

Conclusion

Parents and religious educators should regularly discuss with children the meaning of the eucharist in terms that the children can grasp and apply to their own life situation. All of this can and should happen gradually, as children develop and grow in the various ritual competencies discussed above. Just as the child Jesus went to the Temple to learn more about God's ways, so must we help the children entrusted into our care to learn about the love of that same God as they come to worship in God's house. In the mystery of the eucharist, they encounter divine love in a unique and powerfully transformative way. May our efforts support, not block, their discovery of that love, so that they may—like the child Jesus—grow in wisdom and grace.